Robert D. Weitz
Editor

Psycho-Economics: Managed Care in Mental Health in the New Millennium

Psycho-Economics: Managed Care in Mental Health in the New Millennium has been co-published simultaneously as *Critical Strategies: Psychotherapy in Managed Care,* Volume 1, Number 1 2000.

Pre-publication
REVIEWS,
COMMENTARIES,
EVALUATIONS . . .

"**T**his is an extraordinary timely endeavor, providing the mental health community with a wide range of views on the highly emotional and quite complex issue of Managed Care. Presently 164 million Americans, approximately 57 percent of our population, are enrolled in Managed Care. Hated by many practitioners and their patients, subject to Congressional and media review; yet, few health policy experts expect Managed Care or provider accountability to 'go away.' The evolving changes we are currently experiencing within our health care system are profound and have major implications for practice, research, and training. The impacts of exponential technological advances are not far behind."

Pat DeLeon
Immediate Past-Recording Secretary
American Psychological Association

More pre-publication
REVIEWS, COMMENTARIES, EVALUATIONS . . .

"There's something for everyone interested in the delivery of psychological services in the managed care environment in *Psycho-Economics: Managed Care in Mental Health in the New Millennium*, edited by pioneering private practitioner, professional school dean, APA activist, and psycho-innovator, Robert D. Weitz. While not unbiased in their assessment of the negative impact of managed care on patients, practitioners, and society, the authors of the diverse chapters in this volume nonetheless manage to do their best to present reasoned, rational, clinically informed estimates of what is, what might have been, and what is destined to be.

Depending on whose point-of-view you choose in this volume, what is, as a result of managed care, is: an unmitigated disaster for quality mental health services (Rogers H. Wright); an irresistible force that has brought many changes to clinical practice, few of them in the best interests of patients (Ron E. Fox, Ken Lessler, and Charles Cooper); or a movement that has brought welcome accountability and responsivity to societal changes, albeit along with serious problems for patients and practitioners (Lisa B. Freudenberger, Herbert J. Freudenberger, and Dorothy Sharlip). What might

have been is poignantly detailed by Nicholas A. Cummings, whose vision of psychologists controlling their own destiny in a time of cost containment and increased demands for accountability might have been but, ultimately, was not to be. What is destined to be is anticipated by a host of authors. Some despair that not much of value to patients and practitioners will remain after managed care has its way. Others, more optimistically, believe that society will ultimately rise up to demand an end to managed care's ravages, in favor of a return to an emphasis on quality care. Still others anticipate that psychologists and social workers will ultimately find a *modus vivendi* with managed care that will permit them to offer their services, at a reasonable cost, to the patients who most need them."

Peter E. Nathan, PhD
Distinguished Professor of Psychology
University of Iowa, Iowa City

More pre-publication
REVIEWS, COMMENTARIES, EVALUATIONS . . .

"**D**enial, while powerful, is not conducive to truly effective problem solving resolution, but mental health professionals have been largely in denial regarding their ultimate fate in this new age of Managed Care (MC). The tragic impact of bottom-line driven service curtailments and professional harassment has impacted every practitioner in one way or another. This important new book, well written by knowledgeable colleagues, confronts us with the increasingly calamitous effects of MC. Although I am a long-time clinician closely involved with professional developments, I still found its contents to be candid, disturbing, and yet enlightening. Every behavioral health practitioner should be acutely aware of the issues and implications discussed in these pages. Only with full and honest knowledge of the profound problems brought about by MC business practices can we begin to cope realistically and effectively with their consequences and possible solutions."

Melvin A. Gravitz, PhD, ABPP
Independent Practice
Washington, DC

"**P**sycho-Economics presents an outstanding review of managed behavioral health. Robert Weitz, the Editor, has selected some of the most articulate spokespersons who delineate the problems facing practitioners since managed care became the dominant force in the provision of health care. The authors are psychologists and social workers. The coverage is sufficiently broad to accommodate such divergent views of Rogers H. Wright and Nicholas Cummings. Practical aspects are found throughout this volume. For example, Ron Fox and his colleagues address the problems of surviving in the era of managed care. Others delineate issues of confidentiality and ethical dilemmas that this system of care imposes on practitioners.

Within the covers of this volume the reader will find a reasoned analysis of managed care and the implications for practice."

Reuben J. Silver, PhD
Professor and Head
Psychology Section
Albany Medical College
Albany, NY

Psycho-Economics:
Managed Care
in Mental Health
in the New Millennium

Psycho-Economics: Managed Care in Mental Health in the New Millennium has been co-published simultaneously as *Critical Strategies: Psychotherapy in Managed Care,* Volume 1, Number 1 2000.

The *Critical Strategies: Psychotherapy in Managed Care* Monographic "Separates"

Below is a list of "separates," which in serials librarianship means a special issue simultaneously published as a special journal issue or double-issue *and* as a "separate" hardbound monograph. (This is a format which we also call a "DocuSerial.")

"Separates" are published because specialized libraries or professionals may wish to purchase a specific thematic issue by itself in a format which can be separately cataloged and shelved, as opposed to purchasing the journal on an on-going basis. Faculty members may also more easily consider a "separate" for classroom adoption.

"Separates" are carefully classified separately with the major book jobbers so that the journal tie-in can be noted on new book order slips to avoid duplicate purchasing.

You may wish to visit Haworth's website at . . .

http://www.haworthpressinc.com

. . . to search our online catalog for complete tables of contents of these separates and related publications.

You may also call 1-800-HAWORTH (outside US/Canada: 607-722-5857), or Fax 1-800-895-0582 (outside US/Canada: 607-771-0012), or e-mail at:

getinfo@haworthpressinc.com

Psycho-Economics: Managed Care in Mental Health in the New Millennium, edited by Robert D. Weitz (Vol. 1, No. 1, 2000). *This informative book gives health care administrators suggestions for the improvement of the managed care system and health care in general. Discussing the public's negative view of managed care as a money-making business, not a health care operation,* Psycho-Economics *rewrites what the goal and aim of a managed care provider should be and what legislators can do to rework the system.*

Psycho-Economics: Managed Care in Mental Health in the New Millennium

Robert D. Weitz, PhD
Editor

Psycho-Economics: Managed Care in Mental Health in the New Millennium has been co-published simultaneously as *Critical Strategies: Psychotherapy in Managed Care,* Volume 1, Number 1 2000.

The Haworth Press, Inc.
New York • London • Oxford

Psycho-Economics: Managed Care in Mental Health in the New Millennium has been co-published simultaneously as *Critical Strategies: Psychotherapy in Managed Care,* Volume 1, Number 1 2000.

The development, preparation, and publication of this work has been undertaken with great care. However, the publisher, employees, editors, and agents of The Haworth Press and all imprints of The Haworth Press, Inc., including The Haworth Medical Press® and Pharmaceutical Products Press®, are not responsible for any errors contained herein or for consequences that may ensue from use of materials or information contained in this work. Opinions expressed by the author(s) are not necessarily those of The Haworth Press, Inc.

The Haworth Press, Inc., 10 Alice Street, Binghamton, NY 13904-1580 USA

Cover design by Thomas J. Mayshock Jr.

Library of Congress Cataloging-in-Publication Data

Psycho-economics : managed care in mental health in the new millennium / Robert D. Weitz, editor.
    p. cm.
    "Has been co-published simultaneously as Critical strategies: psychotherapy in managed care, volume 1, number 1, 2000."
    Includes bibliographical references and index.
    ISBN 0-7890-0780-0 (alk. paper)–ISBN 0-7890-0815-7 (alk. paper)
    1. Managed mental health care–United States. I. Weitz, Robert D. (Robert Daniel)
RC465.6.P787 1999
362.2'0425–dc21
                                                          99-047992

INDEXING & ABSTRACTING

Contributions to this publication are selectively indexed or abstracted in print, electronic, online, or CD-ROM version(s) of the reference tools and information services listed below. This list is current as of the copyright date of this publication. See the end of this section for additional notes.

- *Biology Digest*

- *CNPIEC Reference Guide: Chinese National Directory of Foreign Periodicals*

- *Mental Health Abstracts*

- *OT BibSys*

- *Referativnyi Zhurnal (Abstracts Journal of the All-Russian Institute of Scientific and Technical Information)*

Special Bibliographic Notes related to special journal issues (separates) and indexing/abstracting:

- indexing/abstracting services in this list will also cover material in any "separate" that is co-published simultaneously with Haworth's special thematic journal issue or DocuSerial. Indexing/abstracting usually covers material at the article/chapter level.
- monographic co-editions are intended for either non-subscribers or libraries which intend to purchase a second copy for their circulating collections.
- monographic co-editions are reported to all jobbers/wholesalers/approval plans. The source journal is listed as the "series" to assist the prevention of duplicate purchasing in the same manner utilized for books-in-series.
- to facilitate user/access services all indexing/abstracting services are encouraged to utilize the co-indexing entry note indicated at the bottom of the first page of each article/chapter/contribution.
- this is intended to assist a library user of any reference tool (whether print, electronic, online, or CD-ROM) to locate the monographic version if the library has purchased this version but not a subscription to the source journal.
- individual articles/chapters in any Haworth publication are also available through the Haworth Document Delivery Service (HDDS).

ABOUT THE EDITOR

Robert D. Weitz, PhD, (PsyD, honorary) has been a pioneer of independent clinical practice and a forerunner of the professional school movement in psychology. He has been recognized for his professional advocacy and for his distinguished contributions to applied clinical practice in areas of clinical training and scholarly publication. Dr. Weitz has served the American Psychological Association in a variety of roles throughout his long and productive career, and is currently a fellow of the Association and of Divisions 12 (Clinical), 13 (Consulting), 29 (Psychotherapy), 38 (Health), and 42 (Independent). He was also founding editor of *Psychotherapy in Private Practice* (now the *Journal of Psychotherapy in Independent Practice*), and has been awarded diplomate status in Clinical Psychology (ABPP) and in Clinical Hypnosis (ABPH). After participating in the founding of Nova Southeastern University, Dr. Weitz currently serves as Professor Emeritus and as a member of the Center for Psychological Studies Advisory Board.

Psycho-Economics: Managed Care in Mental Health in the New Millennium

CONTENTS

Introduction

I have been honored by The Haworth Press with their invitation to serve as editor of this special volume, *Psycho-Economics: Managed Care in Mental Health in the New Millennium*. Following my acceptance of this role, I invited highly qualified psychologists to express their views concerning managed care for publication in this collection. The resulting articles are presented in the pages which follow. Through consultations with the series editor, Frank De Piano, and the publisher, Bill Cohen, I learned of the philosophy and goals of this volume's companion journal, *Critical Strategies: Psychotherapy in Managed Care*. These are listed below:

- To bring practitioners innovative and effective approaches to clinical practice in relation to managed care.
- To serve as a survival guide in helping the contemporary practitioner maintain an ethical and effective practice while coping with the administrative expectations of the managed care system.
- To foster awareness of the means by which managed care affects the quality of care provided to the patient.
- To foster awareness of the steps that can be taken to minimize the negative affects that managed care dictates on patient care and professional practice in general.
- To foster awareness of the ethical and legal considerations which must be of concern to the providers of mental health services.
- To encourage discussion of the future of the managed care system with regard to the impact upon providers and patients.

While it is the intent of the editor and the publisher to be even-handed in publishing pro and con articles regarding managed care, it is the

[Haworth co-indexing entry note]: "Introduction." Weitz, Robert D. Co-published simultaneously in *Critical Strategies: Psychotherapy in Managed Care* (The Haworth Press, Inc.) Vol. 1, No. 1, 2000, pp. 1-2; and: *Psycho-Economics: Managed Care in Mental Health in the New Millennium* (ed: Robert D. Weitz) The Haworth Press, Inc., 2000, pp. 1-2. Single or multiple copies of this article are available for a fee from The Haworth Document Delivery Service [1-800-342-9678, 9:00 a.m. - 5:00 p.m. (EST). E-mail address: getinfo@haworthpressinc.com].

1

opinion of this editor that this goal will be difficult to maintain in view of the negative public image of the managed care system. How can managed care be accepted by the public when it functions as a money-making business? How can managed care be accepted when it is offered as a commodity on Wall Street? How can managed care be accepted when its officers receive yearly millions of dollars in salaries and bonuses? How can managed care be accepted when patients are denied needed treatment on the grounds that the treatment is experimental? How can managed care be accepted when patients are forced to leave the hospital when their conditions warrant continued inpatient care? How can managed care be accepted when mental health patients are limited to two or three therapeutic visits when they may require several more sessions for successful treatment? In short, how can the concept of managed care, as it presently exists, be publicly accepted when the aim of its management is to gain profits at the expense of the patients?

As the saying goes, "What goes around, comes around." It is the opinion of this writer that, in due time, the public will react with sufficient intensity to stimulate national legislation which will bring about marked changes in the current operation of the system or, perhaps, discard the system in favor of another method to the approach of providing health care for the public.

Robert D. Weitz, PhD, ABPP, ABPH
Diplomate in Clinical Psychology
Diplomate in Psychological Hypnosis

The Health Care Market: Money Wins, You Lose

Lewis W. Field, PhD, ABPP

The promise was there
For all of managed care
But do figures add up
With shortcuts here
and shortcuts there?

The patient is lost
Priced out by buy-outs
Big money wins and
Little patients lose
With confidentiality breached
And confidence capitulated
The Blue Chip price on your head and mine
Is a Dow-Jones bust
In the health care market.

Lewis W. Field is a Diplomate in Clinical Psychology.
Address correspondence to: Lewis W. Field, PhD, 6001 Blackhorse Pike, #31, Egg Harbor Township, NJ 08401-4804.

[Haworth co-indexing entry note]: "The Health Care Market: Money Wins, You Lose." Field, Lewis W. Co-published simultaneously in *Critical Strategies: Psychotherapy in Managed Care* (The Haworth Press, Inc.) Vol. 1, No. 1, 2000, p. 3; and: *Psycho-Economics: Managed Care in Mental Health in the New Millennium* (ed: Robert D. Weitz) The Haworth Press, Inc., 2000, p. 3. Single or multiple copies of this article are available for a fee from The Haworth Document Delivery Service [1-800-342-9678, 9:00 a.m. - 5:00 p.m. (EST). E-mail address: getinfo@haworthpressinc.com].

Managed Care and the Delivery of Psychological Services: An Unmitigated Disaster for Quality Mental Health Services

Rogers H. Wright, PhD

SUMMARY. Managed care and its impact on the delivery of psychological services is evaluated from the perspective of forty plus years of independent practice, and from a knowledge base acquired as a management consultant, designer and operator of service review systems, supervisor of professional liability insurance programs and as a designee and director of national political action programs. *[Article copies available for a fee from The Haworth Document Delivery Service: 1-800-342-9678. E-mail address: getinfo@haworthpressinc.com <Website: http://www.haworthpressinc.com>]*

KEYWORDS. Managed care, mental health, independent practice, private practice

This article is written from the perspective of one of those psychologists who pioneered in full-time independent delivery of psychological services. Along the way, I was privileged to participate in the political process at state and national levels aimed at gaining licensure

---

Dr. Wright retired on December 31, 1996 as Executive Director of Association for the Advancement of Psychology. He lives in Spring Valley, California.

[Haworth co-indexing entry note]: "Managed Care and the Delivery of Psychological Services: An Unmitigated Disaster for Quality Mental Health Services." Wright, Rogers H. Co-published simultaneously in *Critical Strategies: Psychotherapy in Managed Care* (The Haworth Press, Inc.) Vol. 1, No. 1, 2000, pp. 5-18; and: *Psycho-Economics: Managed Care in Mental Health in the New Millennium* (ed: Robert D. Weitz) The Haworth Press, Inc., 2000, pp. 5-18. Single or multiple copies of this article are available for a fee from The Haworth Document Delivery Service [1-800-342-9678, 9:00 a.m. - 5:00 p.m. (EST). E-mail address: getinfo@haworthpressinc.com].

5

and autonomy for psychologists, reimbursement of psychologists by third party payors, etc. I also had the opportunity to help direct major national insurance plans including health plans; to help develop and operate the country's only databased professional service review plan for mental health service delivery; and to direct the operation of a major public policy organization primarily concerned with mental health issues. I also had opportunities to teach, to supervise, and to do research in some of the more pressing clinical issues. It is from the experience and knowledge base of those years that this evaluation of Managed Care (MC) is written.

My first proposition is that MC can be viewed as a sequential development in a healthcare delivery system that has been out of control almost from its inception. To those colleagues sufficiently uninformed as to believe that the solution to the problem of health care delivery lies in what has been called a "single payor" (i.e., govern-mental system), I opine that such a belief is both without historic support (including the Canadian system currently in very serious economic trouble), and overlooks the fact that the *governmental bureaucracy* and our *political system* are primary contributors to the lack of control. In brief, projections as to utilization (i.e., the consumption of health services) have been historically and consistently inaccurate because they under-predict the absolute consumption of such services and the cost thereof. Consequently, the history of health care service delivery plans (both private and governmental) is one of consistent cost overruns followed by rising costs. The only "cures" for such "premium creep/inflation" were to increase cost and/or reduce the quality/quantity of available health service. Until the advent of managed care with its attendant and specifically created mythologies, any "economies" were difficult to realize, especially given the culture's political commitment to ever-increasing numbers of those "insured"; (i.e., citizens covered by health insurance programs by both governmental and private sector opportunists attempting to reconcile increased demands for health services from ever-increasing numbers of consumers attempting to avail themselves of such services).

Managed care is a logical extension of cost controlling efforts initially touted by the governmental health care bureaucracy and the health insurance industry alike as a means of controlling cost *by diminishing over-utilization* (while, of course, maintaining quality health service delivery). The new (MC) approach would all too quickly demonstrate that it was neither. To anyone with a modicum of experience/knowledge of the realities of health care delivery economics and uncompromised by governmental or corporate "bottomlines," such a fanciful account of health care economics has always sounded remarkably like the claims of a "door to door" salesman with lots of vacuum cleaners to sell.

I also propose that the only real contributions of MC to health service delivery have been the creation and enrichment of a new class of "robber barons" characterized by an almost psychopathic disregard for the well-being of the consumers with whom they had contracted to provide health services. As this article is written, that merry band of thieves known as the MC industry is engaged in an all out battle to prevent the United States Congress from passing a "Patient Bill of Rights" that would among other things mandate (1) a more fulsome disclosure to the consumer of the actual services the company will provide; (2) consumer access to second/specialist opinion; and (3) perhaps, most importantly, holding MC companies and their operators legally responsible for the consequences of their actions. Great is the wailing of the paid "spokespersons" for the managed care companies as to the dangers of increased cost, unlimited litigation, etc., etc. Yet it is this same industry that required congressional action to stop such practices as drive-thru mastectomies and daycare deliveries.

But what of the specific impacts of the practices of MC companies on the delivery of psychological services? To fully understand the deleterious impact of these practices, one must at first at least minimally define what is involved in the delivery of quality psychological services. To this writer, the primary components of high quality psychodiagnostic and/or psychotherapeutic endeavor is commitment to the development of a healthier, better informed, more knowledgeable, more INDEPENDENT consumer. These goals are effected by the formation of a therapeutic dyad where psychological services–including quality psychodiagnostic services–are provided by a highly trained and competent practitioner. The American Psychological Association's (APA) Code of Ethics instructs that the provider's first responsibility is to the consumer, that conflicts of interest are to be avoided or made explicit, that confidentiality is to be respected, and that the consumer is to be kept informed at all times of any information relevant to the pursuit of the psychological contract.

Thus this writer proposes that one or more of the fairly common practices found in MC's mental health service delivery demands of the professional psychologist behavior that is, at best, marginally unethical: and, in many instances, constitutes a blatant violation of one or more of the APA's principles of ethics. Professional psychological service delivery under a managed care regime will be discussed in the following areas: the therapeutic dyad and professional service delivery; confidentiality; the quantity and quality of psychological services delivered in the MC environment; and the training of providers.

THE THERAPEUTIC DYAD
AND PSYCHOLOGICAL SERVICE DELIVERY

Perhaps one of the most, if not the most, devastating impacts of managed care on the delivery of psychological services has been its impact on the therapeutic dyad, an impact defined by a shift in the behaviors of the participants and of the way in which information is exchanged. Whereas APA's Code of Ethics instructs psychologists as to the importance of full disclosure, the practices of most managed care companies, at best, is to encourage guarded disclosure; and many demand of their providers the outright withholding of critical information. The most immediate and flagrantly violative example thereof is that situation in which part of the provider's compensation is determined by "bonuses" based on conformity to an acceptable provider profile and/or a baseline for consumption; that is to say, the provider's income is determined not by the quality of delivered service but by how closely the amount of provided service matches a baseline derived in some undisclosed fashion by a party at interest (the MC company). MC companies rationalize this practice on the basis that it sensitizes the provider to the importance of over-utilization thereby making delivered service "medically necessary" and maximally economic. In truth, such arrangements result in strong pressures on the professional to provide minimal professional service. It almost goes without saying that the consumer/subscriber is rarely informed of such "consumer *UN*friendly" contractual agreements. In far too many MC settings, the consumer is equally uninformed about the range of treatment options which may be relevant to amelioration of the presenting condition. Literature, both professional and popular, documents that in a significant number of instances the withholding of treatment (e.g., hospitalization, protective environment) have resulted in homicides and suicides perpetrated by the despairing consumer. In such a "Father knows best; we'll tell you when you should know" environment, efforts to build independence, assertiveness, the exercise and acceptance of responsibility for making informed consumer judgements can only be sorely compromised.

Another problematic consequence of MC service delivery is the redefinition of the therapeutic dyad from one which emphasizes the equality of the participants and the importance of consumer independence and autonomy to one in which the role relationship more closely approximates the so-called "medical model" (wherein the provider enjoys knowledge not available to the consumer) thereby encouraging passivity, dependence, and subservience on the part of the consumer.

Concurrently MC interjects a third party (the payor) into the treatment relationship now making the therapeutic dyad a triad. A legitimate argument has been made that whenever a third party is paying for the cost of delivered health service, that party has a right to such information as is necessary to justify approval for payment of a claim. But the immediate consequence of such "payor" participation is that the therapeutic process now incorporates a third party whose interest is, in most cases, opposed, if not directly antithetical, to those of the consumer and provider. In past years when "fee for service" health care delivery predominated, the intrusion of the third party was generally restricted to requesting limited information from the provider which a claims manager could then process according to the contractual agreements incorporated in the health plan contract. In the main, this system worked relatively well because relatively limited information was needed for claims processing and/or because the third party payor had the prescience to spell out in contractual form the nature and *extent* of the benefit to be provided. Even though in the foregoing context, the intrusion of the third party was generally minimal, it produced a not too subtle shift in the nature of the relationship and obligations of provider to consumer; i.e., it made the provider in effect responsible for insuring that the consumer's claim would be honored, an important shift in emphasis which under any circumstances also tends to increase the passivity and dependency of the consumer and insure a diminution in the consumer's autonomy. Although, it may be politically incorrect to say so, many providers have long felt that *any* third party payment substantially diminishes consumer motivation to change.

However, given that "fee-for-service" still continued to dominate health care delivery, third party payors continued to struggle with their actuarial inaccuracies (i.e., under-projecting the rate of consumption), but third party payors as a class demanded ever yet more stringent controls on the consumption of health services. Thus was born Peer Review and/or Utilization Review which ostensibly was to protect the third party payor against over-utilization of health care services while insuring the consumer of high quality in the delivered service. The immediate consequence of this type of intrusion was a further modification in the role relationship wherein the third party payor gained some apparent additional control (on the consumption of health services) while the provider was further burdened with responsibility for procuring review approval; and the consumer's responsibility was lessened. Furthermore, the law of unintended consequences was manifestly at work because the various changes also placed consumer and provider in a cooperative effort to get the third party to pay for the consumer's utilization of the professional's services.

Peer/utilization review also introduced yet another dimension of change in that it legitimized second-guessing (by representatives of the third party) of the decisions made by the consumer and provider as to utilization; while "desensitizing" all concerned to the fact that peer/utilization review was a further intrusion into the realm of confidentiality because consumer/provider was required to supply ever more substantial and intimate detail about the presenting problem, the treatment process, etc., to the third party.

Even so, it rapidly became apparent to third party payors that despite its substantial intrusion into the treatment process, peer/utilization review when well and appropriately done was not economically effective in controlling cost. The American Psychological Association's (APA's) costly adventure into peer review made clear that when poorly done, peer/utilization review could also have a substantial deleterious impact on the consumption of mental health services. Parenthetically, the resultant complete redesign of the APA program (based on clinical practice, research data from peer reviews efforts, etc.) resulted in a reasonably tolerable program, but the new program was both time consuming from the standpoint of the consumer/provider and expensive from the standpoint of the third party payor. Realistically, and perhaps most importantly, the experience with utilization/peer review made clear that while these efforts to control utilization still did not provide a level of cost control acceptable to third party payors, the practices and procedures pioneered by peer/ professional service review did provide a precedent for the ultimate emergence of managed care.

Before looking further at the emergence and the impact of managed care per se, it is worthwhile to note again that the above described evolutionary process has resulted in the role relationship between provider and consumer shifting from one in which the consumer had full control of all decisions (relative to the consumption of psycho-diagnostic and psychotherapeutic services) to one in which the third party is the only truly autonomous participant. Furthermore, these shifts in the therapeutic triad resulted in a substantial, if not outright loss, of therapeutic distance between provider and consumer with deleterious consequence to both.

Now comes "Managed Care," a system that claims great savings for third party payors while maintaining a high quality of service. However, nothing is said of the fact that the system also codified a "father knows best" approach to the delivery of mental health services while institutionalizing the disincentives embodied in a situation where the third party has the ultimate power of decision. In this system, consumer and provider literally do not know when a given service will be approved or disapproved; and, if approved, for how much, nor for how long. The immediate impact on the consumer is the *IM*possibility of any long range planning either with respect to the further consumption of mental health care services and/or the economic consequence of denial (of payment) for those already consumed. (Most MC claims review was initially retrospective.) The MC system also generally requires of the provider that a "treatment plan" be submitted for claims review, a plan incorporating projected goals and a description of the procedures to be utilized in reaching the goals. Such a process presumes that a third party reviewer is competent to evaluate and/or approve the treatment plan. In virtually no instance were provisions made by MC company for the inclusion of the consumer in this so-called "treatment planning process" nor were any provisions made to insure the competency of the third party payor's reviewer; e.g., that they have even a minimal level of competence, let alone a level of competence comparable to that of the provider. In sum, the evolved MC system treats the consumer as if they were an incompetent malingerer with no rights nor needs; and treats the provider as a scheming crook whose primary intent is disadvantaging the pocketbook of the benevolent third party payor.

A "time coincidental" and unfortunate Supreme Court interpretation of the Employees Retirement Income and Security Act (ERISA) removed the third party payors in MC from any oversight by state health regulatory agencies and shielded them from civil liability for the consequences of their actions. The same Court decision also allowed third party payors (e.g., health insurance companies) and/or their agents to enter directly into the field of service provision, a situation in which such entities enjoyed the same freedom from regulation and/or civil responsibility for their actions. Consequently, the health insurance industry directly or through its agents in MC companies are now simultaneously in the business of insuring the delivery of a health care service; while providing that same service under their own conditions and with little responsibility to anyone other than their stockholders. Thus insurance companies have become the "super provider" of health services purveyed through the medium of their own employees and/or provider panels which must, as do their own employees MC-(HMO), conform to policies, procedures, and standards established by the parent company.

This set of circumstances has further changed the traditional provider role to one in which the professional is primarily responsible to the MC company and only secondarily responsible to the consumer. In this system, the provider's well-being now rests on the degree to which the participating provider can meet the standards imposed by the employer and/or the standards imposed to maintain participation in the MC provider panel. It also puts the provider squarely in the middle between the managed care company's standards, procedures, etc., and a malpractice action from a dissatisfied consumer (i.e., nothing in the earlier noted Supreme Court decision on ERISA relieved the *provider* from the liability attendant to the responsibility for patient care). To say the very least, the participating provider must have a high tolerance for anxiety attendant to the constant knowledge of marginally or wholly unethical conduct; or the provider must have a substantial psychopathic element in his character structure that enables functioning in such a setting.

CONFIDENTIALITY

Due to the excellent work of Dr. Karen Shore and her colleagues who formed the National Coalition of Mental Health Professionals and Consumers, the impact of managed care on confidentiality of psychodiagnostic and psychotherapeutic data has been well delineated, a documentation which suggests that impact of MC practices and procedures is highly deleterious. Little can be added to the comprehensive work of Dr. Shore and her colleagues; and the reader is referred to her group's numerous publications on the subject of confidentiality.

From this writer's perspective, it is possible that too much has been made of the issue of confidentiality in that it has often been presented as the pre-eminent concern about MC. As a psychologist in training in the Veteran's Administration during the lamented "McCarthy" years, I am all too familiar with the sensitivity of and the abuses which can be visited on confidential data.

However, our culture has changed greatly, and data once thought highly sensitive is commonplace in today's discourse. It is arguable that some of the time some of the anxiety about confidentiality is a provider variable which gets communicated to the consumer. From this writer's perspective, concerns about confidentiality in the MC environment, though certainly legitimate, must not so dominate our perspective as to diminish our sensitivity to other major problems inherent in the MC process.

In summary, it is important to note that the voluminous and detailed documentation demanded by companies becomes a part of a corporate or governmental databank stored in computers. The media regularly details the uses–and misuses–of such databases, and the same media also documents that such data is in no sense secure.

QUALITY AND QUANTITY OF CARE

The assaults of MC service delivery on the psychodiagnostic and psychotherapeutic process and on confidentiality as detailed above can only result in a diminution of the quality of health services delivered under such circumstances. However, these effects, irrespective of their significance (or lack thereof) in reducing cost, are in the main coincidental as compared to the direct cost cutting efforts of MC companies. The plain fact is that the major way in which managed care companies control cost is through direct limitations on the amount of care provided. The ingenuity of MC companies in creating disincentives to the utilization of mental health services is impressive: ranging from so convoluting the process that the patient becomes exhausted or disgusted long before treatment is initiated; to procedures requiring "prior authorization" for all rendered services–prior authorization that is limited to one to three sessions at a time.

With respect to psychodiagnostics, many companies employ a series of approved "tests" (a formulary which although by no means necessarily the best means of investigating the presenting problem are most assuredly the simplest and therefore the cheapest). Because of the cost factor, inpatient care is strenuously discouraged, if not altogether prohibited. Provider utilization profiles based on the absolute amount of service delivered, unleavened by a consideration of the nature of the presenting problem, are yet another all too common attempt to control cost. Inasmuch as provider compensation and/or continuance on a MC provider list is dependent on conformity with "utilization guidelines," "provider profiles," etc., the direct impact is to diminish the amount of care provided; and the limitation of such care as is provided to essentially supportive or so-called "crisis" intervention strategies.

Another MC practice that substantially impacts the quality of care is the use of "counselors" as the providers of psychodiagnostic and psychotherapeutic services. Given the earlier noted exemptions of many MC programs from regulations by state health care supervisory agencies, and their widespread freedom from civil liability, results in MC companies going outside the ranks of the traditionally recognized mental health providers (such as psychologists, psychiatrists, psychiatric social workers); substituting therefor marginally qualified, frequently uncredentialed, "mental health counselors."

The foregoing commentary may be interpreted to suggest that MC is altogether responsible for the decline in the quality and quantity of psychotherapeutic services. Such is not the intent, for whereas the practices and procedures of MC companies have certainly made major contributions to an overall decline in the quality and quantity of such services; factors such as "feel good therapies," judicial decisions equating mental health care with physical health care (and thereby relieving consumers from any responsibility for the outcome); and the politicization of such things as training, diagnostic categories, preferential treatment for certain types of mental health problems have also made significant contributions thereto.

TRAINING

American Psychology has for years been shooting itself in the foot–and continues to do so–with respect to the training of psychologists, especially those being trained as providers of mental health services. However, MC companies' employment of uncredentialed or subdoctorally credentialed "counselors" provides another weapon so psychology can shoot itself in both feet simultaneously.

The American Psychological Association (APA), dominated almost from its outset by academic psychologists historically, had little interest in defining clinical practice; and even less interest in the statutory regulation thereof. Consequently, any effort to define areas of expertise and clinical practice and/or to define differences in the functioning of psychologists (trained variously as clinical psychologists, consulting psychologists, experimental psychologists, etc.) were and still are being resisted within psychology's major national organization. The consequent lack of leadership at a national level with respect to the control of professional practice resulted in various state psychological associations assuming leadership roles in seeking legislative regulation of the practice of psychology, a development which further complicated matters because it was broadly felt that "all" psychologists within a given state should both support and be "covered" by projected legislation. The result was a hodgepodge of legislation, which in some states recognized subdoctorally educated providers for limited service provision.

After successful legislative action concerning credentialing in a number of states, APA acceded to the inevitable and undertook a range of activities addressing mental health service delivery by psychologists. Unfortunately, many of APA's positions were politically dictated and/or "split hairs," especially on matters such as training for psychology service providers, etc. As a case in point, APA adopted as policy the position that whereas a doctorate degree constituted "the journeyman level" for independent service providers, subdoctoral training was adequate for service provision in an "institutional" setting. Attempting to rationalize the apparent discrepancy, the APA noted that the subdoctorally trained would be "supervised" in an institutional setting. The consequences of such a policy, e.g., the establishment of a "tiered" mental health system, were not and have not been addressed, nor were the ethics of academics who operated subdoctoral training programs in states where there was no recognition of the subdoctorally trained. However, governmental mental health agencies free from regulatory constraints did employ such "counselors" in significant numbers.

Unfortunately, APA also made few consistent efforts to encourage compliance with its enunciated policies. Although, the politics of this situation is historically fascinating, its full consequence in this context was not apparent until the emergence of managed care.

With its primary emphasis on cost containment and the virtual absence of regulatory controls of health care providers in the MC environment, subdoctorally trained providers of all persuasions, including those in psychology, found an opening to the marketplace not previously enjoyed. Predictably, MC companies began to employ subdoctorally trained mental health providers in significant numbers, a development resulting in increased interest in the operation of subdoctorally training programs in psychology. This sequence of events (elsewhere referenced as the "over-production of the under-qualified") resulted in yet further unsuccessful efforts to gain APA acceptance and approval of subdoctoral training programs as a legitimate terminal training exercise. With MC companies' emergence as a primary provider, a very recent and altogether not unexpected circumstance has been the emergence of academic training programs in psychology tailored specifically to the production of providers trained to function "in the managed care environment."

The manifest contradiction between a national organization demanding of its members conformity to the highest ethical standards in their independent practice and the apparent willingness of APA to tolerate the activities of many of its academic members engaging in training enterprises which subvert those ethical standards and/or encourage participation in situations in which there are direct violations of APA's ethical code, has yet to be resolved.

PROFESSIONAL INTEGRITY
IN A MANAGED CARE SETTING

It is difficult to understand how mental health practitioners, particularly psychologists, can function in a health care delivery setting which treats patients like a popular "recipe" for growing mushrooms, all the while professing to be maintaining the highest professional standards. MC's commitment to protection of the economic bottom line by its unending use of disincentives to consumption and its out-right denial of patient mental health care has so truncated the delivery of quality mental health services and so delimited the role of the mental health care provider as to turn participating providers into little more than paid "friends or companions." Perhaps our academic col-leagues have it right after all, for what provider-to-be in *their right mind* is likely to invest the time, effort, and expense of getting quality training when the utilization of such training requires subordination to or is proscribed by so-called practice guidelines, pseudo "outcome studies," and/or participation in a type of mental health service deliv-ery that is defined by an actuarial table.

Having followed (and opposed) the extremities of MC practice from its inception, I have been privileged to observe that MC's public acceptance (once fairly open) has degenerated, from initial claims to be the Great Savior (of third party subsidized health care delivery), to one of the Great Satan–the butt of unending sarcasm by television talk show commentators, movie commentators, etc. In that period of time, the consuming public is increasingly aware that the sobriquet "MC" is nothing more than a politically acceptable name for a scam in which the inherent conflict of interest between the third party payor and the consumer has been resolved by giving *total control* to the payor. In its journey, MC has attempted to claim service to the public interest by controlling over-utilization and costs–while remaining monumentally silent about the fact that such controls can only be realized in a context in which the health service that the third party payor has contracted to provide *is restricted or not provided at all.* In the furtherance of the goal of not paying claims, MC companies have devised an incredible series of gambits whose intent is to limit service. Outcome studies are all the rage and as many observers have commented simply do not work. In fact, many of them are so poorly designed and/or so limited in application that it reminds this author of a long ago report of a serious study printed in a national psychological journal demonstrat-ing that the Rorschach test was not a good selector of prison guards. As psychologists well know, the use of actuarial techniques certainly has a valid place in projecting the incidence of a given condition in a large population. However, psychologists also well know that the use of such actuarial data to govern specific management in a given case is a misuse of the statistical technique; as is the use of provider profiles absent a specific reference to the caseload of the individual provider.

From my following of this troubled history, I have yet to find serious and/or research data supporting the proposition that MC is really "good for the consumer." Rather I have heard endless defenses of managed care procedures in the context of "it saves money, it prevents over-utilization," etc., etc., etc. Nor have I heard any credible statements supporting the existence of quality care in such a setting. Based on my experience and knowledge, I rather strongly doubt that it exists. Meanwhile what about the integrity and ethics of those psychologists who participate in such practices?

The First Decade
of Managed Behavioral Care:
What Went Right and What Went Wrong?

Nicholas A. Cummings, PhD, ScD

SUMMARY. The first decade of the industrialization of behavioral healthcare provided several spectacular accomplishments as well as a number of unfortunate mistakes. Most disappointing was the industry's loss of clinical focus, resulting in managed *costs* rather than managed *care*. This industrialization followed the pattern seen in all previous courses of industrialization, except the schedule was greatly accelerated in keeping with the rapidity of the current information age. A number of predictions can be made as to the evolution of managed behavioral care, as this industrialization is still in its relative infancy. The practitioner who anticipates that managed behavioral care will simply go away and behaves accordingly will experience a dubious future. *[Article copies available for a fee from The Haworth Document Delivery Service: 1-800-342-9678. E-mail address: getinfo@ haworthpressinc.com <Website: http://www.haworthpressinc.com>]*

KEYWORDS. Managed care, independent practice, private practice

---

Nicholas A. Cummings is president of the Foundation for Behavioral Health, chair of The Nicholas & Dorothy Cummings Foundation, Distinguished Professor at the University of Nevada (Reno), and a former president of the American Psychological Association. He founded the first managed behavioral healthcare delivery system, American Biodyne, which later became MedCo/Merck, then Merit, and is now part of Magellan.

[Haworth co-indexing entry note]: "The First Decade of Managed Behavioral Care: What Went Right and What Went Wrong?" Cummings, Nicholas A. Co-published simultaneously in *Critical Strategies: Psychotherapy in Managed Care* (The Haworth Press, Inc.) Vol. 1, No. 1, 2000, pp. 19-37; and: *Psycho-Economics: Managed Care in Mental Health in the New Millennium* (ed: Robert D. Weitz) The Haworth Press, Inc., 2000, pp. 19-37. Single or multiple copies of this article are available for a fee from The Haworth Document Delivery Service [1-800-342-9678, 9:00 a.m. - 5:00 p.m. (EST). E-mail address: getinfo@haworthpressinc.com].

19

As a columnist, I've found that giving people information may not work when they want emotional vindication. As the growing emphasis on feelings crowds out reason, facts will play a smaller role in public discourse.

Paul Craig Roberts, *Business Week, May 25, 1998, p. 22*
John M. Olin Fellow, Institute for Political Economy
Washington, D.C.

The entire field of healthcare has changed dramatically since the initial, unheeded warnings to the profession that behavioral healthcare was about to industrialize (Cummings, 1986; Cummings & Fernandez, 1985). The professions of psychotherapy are still reeling from the magnitude of the change that has occurred in this first wave (1985-1995) and are ill-prepared for the second wave of industrialization that is already underway. The changes that are about to occur will dwarf those of the past decade, and a critical understanding of the course and consequences of industrialization is important if any semblance of independent practice is to survive. This article will address past events and attempt an assessment of the future, even though a bruised and beleaguered profession may not yet be ready for such a reality check.

AN ASSESSMENT OF THE PRESENT

Who Are the Winners?

Those Who Pay the Bills

The undisputed winners in the first wave of the industrialization of healthcare are those who pay the bills: employers, insurers, the federal government (which is the largest purchaser of healthcare in the world), and ultimately the American taxpayer. In the early 1980s the inflationary spiral of healthcare was out of control at a figure two to three times that of the economy in general. When Congress enacted the concept of Diagnosis Related Groups (DRGs), the rate of inflation for medicine and surgery relatively quickly settled at 8% from its previously consistent figure of 12%, while mental health and chemical dependency treatment (MH/CD), which was excluded from DRGs because no one knew how to include them, skyrocketed to 16% annual inflation rate. Suddenly, and for the first time in history, MH/CD was driving the inflationary spiral for all of healthcare. The response of third party payers was swift and potentially devastating: desperate and not knowing what else to do, they began to limit mental health benefits, and even exclude them altogether. The MH/CD benefits for which the public and the profession had fought hard over decades to achieve were in danger of disappearing.

The government essentially left the behavioral health problem to the private sector as it was at a loss as to what legislation might provide a solution. Instead, it facilitated the rapid emergence of private behavioral healthcare companies by ignoring outmoded laws and regulations, such as those limiting the corporate practice of medicine. A few entrepreneurial companies were formed, and as market acceptance and government encouragement were assured, there was a rapid proliferation of behavioral managed care organizations (MBCOs). These came to be known as "carve-outs" because MH/CD was contractually carved out of the existing over-all health benefit into a separate company that was capitated and went at risk for the MH/CD portion of healthcare delivery.

The Healthcare System

The result of this rapid industrialization of healthcare, and particularly behavioral healthcare, was that the health system was saved from bankruptcy. The inflationary rate of healthcare was tethered to a surprising 4.4% by 1996, the lowest it has been since 1960, with a comparable and equally remarkable rate for behavioral healthcare (*Wall Street Journal*, 1998). The credit for saving the system goes to managed care.

That managed care saved the health system is grudgingly acknowledged, but it remains unappreciated that the MBCOs saved the mental health benefit from regressing to its pre-1960s state when no insurer included psychotherapy as a covered benefit. A profession seething from the decimation of its practice is understandably blind to the fact that in the late 1980s the trend which abolished MH/CD as an insured benefit was rapidly gaining momentum and threatened its extinction within a few years. The MBCOs, by capping MH/CD costs and assuming all risks literally saved the behavioral health benefit in America. The solo practitioner of psychotherapy, though hard hit by managed behavioral care, would have been totally out of business were it not for the MBCOs they understandably despise.

Who Are the Losers?

The Psychiatric Hospital

In 1985 Wall Street regarded the psychiatric hospitals as a growth industry. DRGs had an immediate impact on the general hospitals that experienced a drastically reduced bed occupancy rate of as much as 50%. Enterprising hospital administrators, noting there were no DRGs in psychiatry and chemical dependency, converted these empty beds to MH/CD services and huckstered them on television. The 28 day stay for chemical dependency became standard, adult psychiatric hospitalization doubled, and adolescent psychiatric hospitalization quadrupled. This was a clear demonstration of why the economic laws of supply and demand have never applied to healthcare: the provider controls both supply and demand. Investors, believing the boom would last forever, poured money into the psychiatric hospital industry. Huge chains of proprietary psychiatric hospitals were created, and such stocks as Charter Hospitals, Community Psychiatric Centers, and Psychiatric Institutes of America became the darlings of Wall Street. Psychiatric hospitalization was out of control and threatened the stability of the entire healthcare system.

The boom was short-lived. The MBCOs directed their immediate attention to the run-away MH/CD hospitalization rate and applied their most draconian solutions. Seemingly overnight, hospital admissions and lengths-of-stay plummeted, psychiatric hospitals began to lose money, and increased MH/CD admissions as a solution to the general hospitals' economic dilemma vanished. To this day the general hospital remains a marginal economic entity, while the psychiatric hospital is seen as an outright economic liability. Many have partnered with physicians to form a kind of managed care company of their own, the so-called Physician Hospital Organization (PHO), with varying degrees of success.

The Private Solo Practitioner of Psychotherapy

The impact on the privately practicing psychotherapist took somewhat longer to become apparent, but it was no less devastating. During the repeated warnings that practice was about to be negatively impacted, psychologists and social workers were experiencing the period of their greatest economic success for two reasons: (1) psychiatry had remedicalized and abandoned psychotherapy to the non-medical psychotherapist, and (2) they were receiving a bonanza of referrals for outpatient follow-up for the unprecedented numbers of hospitalized patients. They were in no mood to hear predictions of doom and gloom. So even after their practices began to dwindle, these practitioners remained in a state of denial. By 1997, however, it had become apparent that the methods the MBCOs were using to pay practitioners (a series of reduced negotiated fees, utilization review, precertification, case management, treatment plans, therapist profiling) had reduced the incomes of privately practicing psychotherapists (*APA Monitor*, 1997).

Although the practitioners were clearly the losers in income, they also suffered the indignity that they were no longer the sole determiners of the treatment process. Accountability, outcomes research, and other factors initiated by the managed care industry demystified what had come to be known as "psychobabble." The payers, having a greater understanding of the treatment process, were no longer timid about disagreeing with, and disregarding the treatment recommendations of the psychotherapists. This loss of professional dignity and autonomy may be greater than loss of income in fomenting practitioner unhappiness. But like the hospitals that no longer determine admissions and lengths of stay, the psychotherapists no longer determine how long psychotherapy should be.

A CRITICAL RETROSPECTIVE

Although a number of very important things went right during the first decade of managed care, the list of things that went wrong is far more extensive. In taking a critical look at both the positives and negatives, it is inevitable that both the opponents and proponents of managed care will be discomfited.

What Went Right?

Healthcare Inflation Was Tethered

This is undoubtedly managed care's greatest accomplishment. To the dismay of those of us who are clinically oriented, it demonstrated for all time that there could be unprecedented cost-containment by merely introducing management into a previously undisciplined practitioner cottage industry. That there are also untoward side-effects to such an industrialization will be discussed below.

Growth

The growth of managed care to the point where it encompassed 75% of the insured market in just a little more than a decade is unprecedented. The managed behavioral care industry accomplished in ten years what the auto industry required fifty years to accomplish, and the airline industry thirty years. This reflects a clear market need that has been met by the MBCO.

Accountability

Managed care has ushered in the era of data-based treatment. The mechanisms that are evolving, although they still have a long way to go, have set the stage for the emergence of treatment guidelines and eventually standardized treatment protocols, all evidence-based. In the meantime, psychotherapists must justify and document treatment plans and outcomes, and goal-oriented therapy has become standard.

The Continuum of Care

A little recognized fact is that managed behavioral care has resulted in the expansion of services as well as an appropriate substitution of services. Not only have both the numbers of persons seeking services and the number of practitioners providing services increased, but psychiatric hospitalization and private practice psychotherapy have both declined in favor of a continuum of care with expanded services. These have included increases in psychiatric rehabilitation, day treatment, consumer-run peer support, residential treatment, and crisis programs. This little known fact is supported by a number of studies conducted in such diverse settings as the Rand Corporation, William A. Mercer, the Institute of Medicine, and Medstat Group, as well as by researchers in prestigious universities which include Harvard, Brandeis, and the University of California at Berkeley (Ross, 1997). While solo practitioners of psychotherapy may find the decline in demand for their services painful, most authorities see the expansion into a continuum as desirable.

Integration and Coordination of Care

In contrast to the non-system that prevailed in private practice for decades, managed care has provided for the first time a vehicle for the coordination of care. It is still admittedly in its infancy, but the potential for increased integration and coordination on a national scale is a possibility.

Self-Regulation

The industry has made rapid strides toward self-regulation, with the National Council for Quality Assurance (NCQA) taking the lead, and the Joint Commission on the Accreditation of Healthcare Organizations (JCHO) soon to follow. Voluntary regulation will undoubtedly make unnecessary some government regulation, but it will not be sufficient to deter all statutory regulation. No industry goes from zero to 75% of the market in a decade without incurring outside regulation.

Value

Defined as price plus quality, value has been difficult to address in healthcare. The American people have come to believe that more is better, permitting the system to provide too much hospitalization, too many prescriptions, unneeded surgeries, and millions of unnecessary procedures because the patient so demands, it benefits the practitioner, or it quells the fear of malpractice in a litigious world. These do not add up to value. Now that healthcare is organized and competitive, the buyer for the first time has the opportunity to address value pricing and the clout to defend it in the legislature, the courts and the marketplace. A recent cost-comparison study by Foster Higgins addresses the relative value of different kinds of health plans. It found that traditional plans have done little to reduce costs, while HMOs have made considerable gains to increase quality, resulting in a widening gap favoring the HMO (Sherer, 1997).

What Went Wrong?

Managing Costs, Not Care: The Loss of Clinical Focus

Managed behavioral care began as a system that managed care through efficient/effective psychotherapy and thereby contained costs through improved care (Cummings, 1988; Cummings & Sayama, 1995). In such a clinical system the practitioners were highly trained in both short-term and long-term therapy, and especially in the need to determine when one or the other is for the benefit of the patient. This eliminated such artificial controls as session limits, utilization review, and case management.

Once practitioners forfeited their initial leadership in managed behavioral healthcare, it was inevitable that the baton would pass to business interests (Cummings, 1986, 1988). It is not expected that business interests would appreciate and comprehend the clinical process, but it does not follow they should be rejecting of it. Perhaps because of fierce hostility from the practitioners, perhaps by sheer expediency, or probably by a combination of both, the industry disregarded the available techniques that contained costs through clinical effectiveness and relied instead on the familiar "bean counters," as insurance actuaries and financial managers are known. Non-clinical judgments are arbitrary and not readily substantiated, giving the industry a less than compassionate image among consumers.

Pricing Pressure

In spite of lofty pronouncements to the contrary, the determining factors in successful behavioral health contracting have been three: price, price and price! The highly competitive atmosphere resulted in companies under-bidding each other in a manner reminiscent of the old fashioned "gas wars." Inevitably, contracts were signed that were below cost, suggesting, at best, that the services promised would never be delivered, or, at worst, that the payer cynically never expected they would be delivered. Competition was so fierce that no company dared declare itself a quality leader, avowing it would never compromise quality by succumbing to destructive price pressure. Insurers, employers and government, elated that inflation was curbed, joined in the frenzy to ratchet down prices even more at the expense of the MBCOs.

The Squeeze on the Providers

Hospitals and practitioners were beginning to accommodate to managed behavioral care when the industry decided to pass on the price pressure by squeezing the providers. Although this was inevitable, the timing was disastrous. Outraged providers joined with consumer groups and national anti-managed care coalitions were formed. With fees already at unprecedented lows, the practitioners seemingly felt they had little else to lose. The disgruntled bear was transformed into a ferocious grizzly.

Loss of the Public Relations Battle

Patients are grateful and loyal to their doctors, not to the health plan. Patient satisfaction studies which separate satisfaction with the doctor from that with the health plan unequivocally reveal this (Hall, 1995). Doctors are rated high while the health plans with which they work are rated much lower, demonstrating that when these variables are not separated, the health plans enjoys a halo effect stemming from patient gratitude toward the practitioner. So when practitioners conveyed their rage at managed care to their patients, the latter became a potent, angry constituency that put pressure on employers, legislators and insurers. A series of television exposes followed, as well as a number of successful movies that portrayed managed care as evil (e.g., *As Good As It Gets*, starring Jack Nicholson).

The loss of the public relations battle has resulted in mounting public pressure that will lead to increased regulation of the managed behavioral healthcare industry. At a time when the industry is besieged by unhealthy competition and shrinking margins, it can little afford the onslaught of public opinion. And it looks on helplessly while its customers (employers, insurers, government) who are responsible for the unhealthy price pressure allow the public to place all the blame on the MBCO.

Competitive Paranoia

At a time when the attacks on the industry required a united front, it is difficult to conceive of anything more destructive than internal paranoia. The American Managed Behavioral Healthcare Association (AMBHA), founded in 1992, has never achieved the strength and prestige that would reflect the size of the industry it represents. Unhealthy competition resulted in MBCOs being distrustful of each other, with each behaving as if it had to guard its "black box." In actuality, there are no black boxes as everyone is essentially doing the same thing. Member companies withdrew from AMBHA for questionable reasons, and there was the added difficulty of members of the AMB-HA board sitting across the table from each other when their respective companies were suing each other.

Opposition to Integration with Primary Care

The carve-in is the very antithesis of the carve-out, and it is not surprising that an industry that has grown to encompass 150 million covered lives and is now fighting for survival would vehemently oppose it. In predicting the industrialization of behavioral care, Cummings (1986) stated the carve-out would be necessary for about a decade. Once the mental health benefit was saved, it would be important for behavioral care to become an integral part of primary care where it belongs. Integration is very likely the second wave in the industrialization of healthcare and much lip service is being paid to the concept. However, the managed behavioral care industry does not understand the concept, fears it, and will likely continue to drag its feet.

What Surprisingly Went Wrong?

In any industrialization there is the inevitable period of chaos that accompanies the transition from the old to the new. This expectation still does not mitigate the pain and discomfort created when old institutions begin to die in favor of the birth of the new order. All of the foregoing accomplishments and mistakes are not surprising and could have been predicted, except possibly for the magnitude and rate of growth. Three occurrences, all viewed by this author as negative and avoidable, were not predicted and are quite surprising. As such they merit special consideration.

The Failure to Change Practice Patterns

The enormous industry we now call managed care has literally turned healthcare upside down. It has decimated practice, it has bankrupted hospitals, it has transferred clinical decision-making from the practitioner to the manager, it has removed the epicenter of healthcare from the hospital to ambulatory care, it has drastically altered payment arrangements, and it has catapulted healthcare from the cottage into an industry. It has altered all kinds of practitioner behavior, but it has miserably failed to change *practice patterns* There is a distinct difference between changes in practitioner behavior and changes in practice patterns, yet the distinction is not easily understood and a simple illustration from medical practice may be helpful.

A managed care company (MCO) requires that all its network physicians prescribe generic drugs. They comply and the MCO calculates the cost savings with this change in behavior. Concurrently, almost every patient diagnosed as suffering from a common cold and demands an antibiotic is prescribed one, even though such a treatment is counter-indicated for a virus. The antibiotics prescribed are generic, however, indicating a change in physician *behavior.* The reason the patient receives the inappropriate, but generic antibiotic is because *practice pattern* requires that each patient be seen for only seven minutes, and it would require twenty minutes to explain to a patient demanding an antibiotic why the physician would not prescribe it. The practice pattern is the seven minute appointment, which determines a number of other behaviors, including the prescribing of an inappropriate, albeit generic antibiotic.

Practice patterns in behavioral health are subtle and pervasive, and the MBCOs have scarcely touched them. Essentially, psychotherapists do what they have always done which is long term psychotherapy, except now they do it in six or ten sessions rather than fifty. They have not honed their skills to include brief, focused or problem-solving approaches, and the result is long-term techniques administered in a brief time frame. The clerical, or paraprofessional case manager who is guided by a company "cookbook" does not really know the difference, and even if he or she were more sophisticated, psychotherapists have been fooling their supervisors for decades. Therapist report is notoriously unreliable, and it is only when psychotherapy is observed directly by sitting in the same room or viewed through a one-way mirror that there is accurate appraisal. Long-term psychotherapy performed in six sessions yields little or no positive results. Consequently, prescriptions for psychotropic drugs skyrocketed in numbers, with small financial comfort that these are, nonetheless, generic.

The early, clinically driven MBCOs trained their therapists in time-sensitive techniques. American Biodyne followed an initial 130 hour training module with a weekly commitment of 15% of clinician time in ongoing training , supervision through direct observation, and clinical case conferencing (Cummings, Pallak & Cummings, 1997). For a time after the MBCOs lost their clinical focus they continued contracting with outside trainers, but this was soon discontinued. Psychotherapists who might commit to rigorous retraining on their own were discouraged from doing so because everyone on the network received the same reduced fee. The MBCOs have altered therapist *behavior* without having impacted *practice patterns*. This is a hidden cost that will eventually surface and result in a round of price increases.

Perpetual Warfare with Its Own Work Force

No industry can long survive when it is at serious odds with its own work force, in this instance the psychotherapist. Commerce is replete with examples of employees who were so enraged with their own employers that they brought them down even though it meant the loss of their own jobs. An unfortunate example was that of Pan American Airlines, until two decades ago the premier air carrier. The flight attendants were so angry at their employer that they systematically set about being rude to the customers until flyers would go out of their way not to fly "Pan Am." At times it seems as if the MBCOs go out of their way to incur the wrath of the practitioner. Their business executives excuse their conduct by pointing to the blind militancy of the professional societies, which behave very much as angry ostriches. This excuse is not valid. Even though the professional societies are governed by an aging group of successful solo practitioners who would rather see the entire system wrecked than to change, the MBCOs have done little or nothing to court the rank-and-file practitioner who experiences nothing but a steady erosion of autonomy, income and dignity, and might respond to an invitation to mutual accommodation.

The MBCOs pride themselves in their skillful marketing, indicating how they have grown to encompass 75% of the insured market. But marketing is both external and internal, and the latter, as it particularly reflects relations with the psychotherapists, has been abysmal. The industry is just now beginning to reap the wild harvest; practitioners have aroused consumers and together they are impacting on employers, insurers and government officials. The outgrowth will be a series of government regulations, an increase in the micro-management of the MBCOs by the purchasers, and an advocacy for patient choice and determination. Unfortunately, all this will result in a new round of price increases.

Merger Mania

The nation is in the grips of merger mania, and perhaps it was inevitable this trend would eventually involve healthcare. However, where it is one thing for banks to be buying each other for purchase prices that seem to defy the laws of gravity, it is unseemly in a "care-giving" industry that until recently was mostly not-for-profit. In predicting the industrialization of healthcare, Cummings (1986) warned that as in all sectors that have industrialized before, there will be a period of consolidation in which the successful companies would buy up the less successful ones, and acquisitions would be used to increase market share. He predicted that by the early 21st Century there would be six to eighteen "megameds" that would control the health industry. He could not have predicted, however, the frenzy that characterized the past few years. The health industry, being business-driven rather than clinically-driven, joined the merger mania that was sweeping Wall Street (Valdmanis, 1998), and it now appears the final number will be closer to six than eighteen. As of this writing one company (Magellan) controls 40% of the market, and with Options which is purchasing Value, just two companies control almost 60% of the market.

It did not seem to matter that margins had grown tissue-paper thin, and several companies were losing money, and servicing company debts had become oppressive; the prices companies were paying to buy each other can be described only as obscene. Magellan's recent acquisition spree has left it with a debt of $1.3 billion, resulting in 15 cents of every revenue dollar being earmarked for debt service (not debt retirement). At a time when not much money is being made in healthcare, and most are losing money, the large profits garnered by a few deal makers leaves the public with the erroneous perception that the managed care industry is greedy and lucrative. This is another public relations battle lost by the industry.

A GLIMPSE AT THE SECOND WAVE OF HEALTHCARE INDUSTRIALIZATION

As practitioners contemplate all of the foregoing, it is no wonder they feel intimidated by managed care. They may be skeptical that, indeed, the second wave in the industrialization of behavioral health-care will bring favorable changes. The fact is, opportunities will emerge rivaling those of the previous decade, but only for those relatively few practitioners who are prepared in attitude, knowledge and skill.

The changes that will occur in the next decade will be as profound as those of the previous decade that left practitioners stunned, angry and impoverished. Now that industrialization has taken place, there is no going back. The purchasers of healthcare have once and for all rested the economic control of the system from the provider, and they will never relinquish that control. But industrialization is a continually evolving process. A few of the trends that will characterize the next decade are beginning to emerge.

Increased Costs

Another round of price increases reminiscent of the early 1980s can be expected for several reasons. The industry is about to find that it has not saved as much money as it thought, and a number of hidden failures are about to surface. Principally is the failure to change prac-tice patterns, and the attendant costs that are imbedded in outmoded ways in which physicians and psychotherapists practice.

Other factors contributing to the next price spiral are (1) increased micro-management of the industry due to consumer demand and nega-tive public opinion, most of which will add costs without improving care; (2) a host of government regulations resulting from the indus-try's having lost the public relations battle, and these will add a bu-reaucratic layer with all the consequent paperwork that will be far more cosmetic than substantive in returning choice and determination to the consumer; and (3) a system of self regulation and accreditation that already promises to be far more successful in accelerating intru-siveness and costs without an equivalent increase in quality.

Integration of Behavioral Health with Primary Care

Recently the federal government and several private sector health contractors (such as the Pacific Business Group) announced contract incentives designed to accelerate the integration of behavioral health with primary care. This is not surprising inasmuch as the "fat" in behavioral health has been successfully wrung out of the system, while the costs of somatizing, as well as stress related and life style related physical conditions, are enormous. Medical cost offset research has demonstrated consistently over thirty years that 5 to 10% savings in medicine and surgery are to be expected with the introduction of behavioral health into primary care (Cummings, 1997a), and the medical cost offset increases with the degree of behavioral/primary care integration. It is startling that a 7% decrease in physical care exceeds the entire MH/CD budget of the United States. A clinically-driven, cost-conscious integrated system is the best way to address such adverse health costs in the future.

A Resurgence of the Practitioner

For the first time in history, healthcare is subject to the forces of supply and demand, and the practitioners who learn this will be successful in their competition with the managed care companies. The future integrated systems will stress local delivery, enabling integrated delivery systems (IDSs) composed of physicians and psychological practitioners to by-pass the MCOs and go directly to the purchasing consortia. The key will be the ability to predict and control costs, enabling an integrated system to accept capitation and go at risk. Behavioral health practitioners who help create these IDSs with physicians can expect to be part of the "physician-equity model" wherein each practitioner is a clinical participant/owner.

The emergence of large, prestigious purchasing consortia has remarkably changed the playing field. Initially formed to give small businesses the same purchasing clout as the large employer by pooling the prospective number of covered lives, these consortia have grown into important buyer/consumer coalitions that have been rapidly educating themselves as to value. The Buyers Health Care Action Group in Minneapolis, which originally believed that costs and quality could best be achieved through mega-MCOs has reversed itself recently. The original buying strategies encouraged the present merger mania, while now this group regards smaller providers with more consumer choice the solution to the next round of price increases (Winslow, 1998). Employer-members of this group are experimenting with giving employees a certain allotment each month with a list of a dozen or more approved provider groups that are rated low, moderate or high cost. The allotment pays for a low cost plan, and an employee has the option of adding personal funds to that figure to obtain a moderate or high cost plan. The group conducts surveys and rates the various plans, revealing that not all high cost plans are rated the highest by the consumer.

These employer strategies, the medical savings accounts currently being debated in the Congress, and the trend toward smaller, local provider groups give the innovative practitioner opportunities that were not available in the previous decade (Cummings, In Press).

The Ever Increasing Glut of Behavioral Care Practitioners Trained for Obsolescence

The greatest threat to the mental health professions has been, and continues to be the constantly increasing number of psychotherapists from a number of separate and often warring professions. These professions (psychology, psychiatry, social work, mental health counselors, marriage/family/child counselors, psychiatric nurse practitioners, masters level psychologists, substance abuse counselors, school or education psychologists, etc.) have yet to define their appropriate relationship to each other and to demonstrate any kind of restraint toward increasing their numbers. MCOs have exploited this glut of practitioners, paying the least acceptable fees which often require a Ph.D. to work for the same fee as a masters level practitioner, whose rate has already been renegotiated downward several times. This failure to come to grips with the practitioner glut has created an insecurity and inter-professional rivalry and rage that some how gets projected onto the MBCO. Victimization is a form of denial which merely prolongs coming to grips with reality.

For but a handful of exceptions, the graduate programs are training practitioners for the pre-industrialized era of healthcare. Students are not prepared for the real world because their cloistered academicians do not have a clue as to what is happening out there. The approvals process in both social work and psychology is remarkably and woefully out of date. Add to this obsolete training the fact there are more psychotherapists in the United States than physicians, and only half of each are really needed, it is surprising the prediction that in the early part of the next century half of those in practice today will not have jobs has been received with such incredulity and hostility (Cummings, Pallak & Cummings, 1996).

The fact that managed care is exploiting this unfortunate state of affairs does not intrinsically make this a managed care problem. The behavioral healthcare professions need to redirect some of the energy that is being expended charging at windmills to begin the enormous task of putting their own houses in order.

CONCLUSION

The first decade of the industrialization of behavioral healthcare has demonstrated a number of spectacular achievements and a larger number of disappointing mistakes. The period of chaos that accompanies the transition from the traditional order to the new mode has a number of facets and is continuing. However, there are indications the first wave in the industrialization of behavioral healthcare is giving way to the second wave which is already in progress.

For a number of reasons practitioners not only missed the first wave in the industrialization of behavioral healthcare, but also in their initial denial and later fury, their professional societies rendered themselves irrelevant to the profound decisions that were being made in American healthcare during the last decade. The nation is at the threshold of the second wave, with the changes that will be even greater than those of the first wave. There is once again opportunity and challenge for the practitioner who can break away from the herd of the practitioner glut by being astute, bold, innovative and visionary. Most practitioners will not rise to the occasion, and the professions for some time to come will continue to produce too many graduates trained for obsolescence. Eventually prospective students will learn there are no jobs in behavioral care and will seek other careers. The professions will then be forced to address the new problem of down-sizing.

The new era favoring the astute practitioner stems from the mistakes the MBCOs have made on the one hand, and the new purchasing arrangements which enable practitioner owned IDSs to by-pass the MCOs and contract directly. The integration of behavioral health with primary care is in its infancy, but promises to profoundly change not only healthcare delivery, but the way behavioral health practitioners practice. The far-sighted practitioners are beginning now to become equity-participants in the health delivery system of the next decade. The future will lie with those practitioners who fill the new roles and who will redefine behavioral health practice.

REFERENCES

Ackley, D. C. (1997). *Breaking free of managed care.* New York: Guilford.

APA Monitor. (1997). Newsline: Practitioners report decrease in earnings. *28*, 3, (March), p. 6.

Cummings, N. A. (1986). The dismantling of our health system: Strategies for the survival of psychological practice. *American Psychologist, 41*, 426-431.

Cummings, N. A. (1988). Emergence of the mental health complex: Adaptive and maladaptive responses. *Professional Psychology: Research and Practice, 19*(3), 308-315.

Cummings, N. A. (1995). Behavioral health after managed care: The next golden opportunity for professional psychology. *Register Report, 20*(3), 1, 30-32.

Cummings, N. A. (1996) the search for capital: Positioning for growth, joint venturing, acquisition, and public offering. In Cummings, N. A., Pallak, M. S., & Cummings, J. L. *Surviving the demise of solo practice: Mental health practitioners prospering in the era of managed care.* Madison, CT: Psychosocial Press, 205-217.

Cummings, N. A. (1997a). Behavioral health in primary care: Dollars and Sense. In Cummings, N. A., Cummings, J. L., & Johnson, J. N., *Behavioral health in primary care: A guide for clinical integration.* Madison, CT: Psychosocial Press, 3-22.

Cummings, N. A. (1997b). Practitioner-driven IDS groups continue as best hope for the future. *National Psychologist,* July/August, 10-11.

Cummings, N. A. (In Press). A Psychologist's proactive guide to managed care: New roles and opportunities. In Kent, A. S. & Hersen, M., *A psychologist's proactive guide to mental health care.* Hillside, N.J.: Lawrence Earlbaum.

Cummings, N. A., Cummings, J. L., & Johnson, J. N. (1997). *Behavioral health in primary care: A guide for clinical integration.* Madison, CT: Psychosocial Press.

Cummings, N. A., & Fernandez, L. (1985). Exciting new opportunities for psychologists in the market place. *Independent Practitioner, 5*, (March), 38-42.

Cummings, N. A., Pallak, M. S., & Cummings, J. L. (1996). *Surviving the demise of solo practice: Mental health practitioners prospering in the era of managed care.* Madison, CT: Psychosocial Press.

Cummings, N., & Sayama, M. (1995). *Focused psychotherapy: A casebook of brief, intermittent psychotherapy throughout the life cycle* . Madison, CT: Psychosocial Press.

Drotos, J. C. (1997). Upheavals in the land of the giants. *Behavioral Health Management, 17*, 8, 39-40.

Edley, R. S. (1996). The practitioner as owner. In Cummings, N. A., Pallak, M. S., & Cummings, J. L., *Surviving the demise of solo practice: Mental health practitioners prospering in the era of managed care.* Madison, CT: Psychosocial Press, 175-190.

Hall, C. T. (1995). Customers rate health plans. *San Francisco Chronicle*, October 25, pp. B1 & B8.

Jeffrey, N. A. (1998). A new balancing act for psychotherapy. *Wall Street Journal*, January 5, B6-7.

Joseph, S. (1997). *Symptom focused psychiatric drug therapy for managed care.* New York: The Haworth Press, Inc.

Oss, M. E. (1997). Business strategy: Foundation for the future. *Behavioral Healthcare Management, 17,* 8 (November/December), 4.

Practice Strategies. (1997). Peaks and valleys. *3,* 12, (December), 1 and 12.

Pullham, S. & Winslow, R. (1997). HMO bleeding is unsettling Wall Street. *Wall Street Journal,* October 9, C1-2.

Ross, E. C. (1997). Plans present mixed bag of results for providers, subscribers. *Tallahassee Democrat,* December 7, F1 and 4.

Ross, C., Covall, M., Graham, M., & Coakley, T. (1998). Experts predict consolidation fall-out, provider-sponsored networks, shrinking behavioral health dollars in 1998. *Managed Behavioral Health News,* January 15, 1-4.

Sherer, R. A. (1997). HMO cost comparison study. *Mental Health Economics, 1,* 1, 1-2.

Sherrid, P. (1997). Mismanaged care? Wall Street takes the scalpel to HMO companies. *U. S. News & World Report,* November 24, 57-62.

Stoil, M. J. (1997). Parity: Case closed? *Behavioral Health Management, 17,* 8, (November/December), 6-7.

Valdmanis, T. (1998). Mega-mergers likely to contain momentum. *USA Today,* January 2, B1 and 6.

Wall Street Journal. (1998). Managed care defenders map an offensive against legislative mandates. January 16, p. 1.

Weinstein, M., & Edley, R. S. (1997). Whither the solo and the group practice? *Behavioral Healthcare Tomorrow, 1,* 6, (February), 39-43.

Winslow, R. (1998). Healthcare inflation revives in Minneapolis despite cost-cutting. *Wall Street Journal,* CXXXVIII, 97 (May 19), pp. A1 & A15.

Professional Problems and Solutions in the Managed Care Era

A. Eugene Shapiro, PhD

SUMMARY. Since World War II the scope of our professional services has grown. The sense of an expanding, increasingly recognized profession came to an end with the emerging dominance of managed care. Psychologists are now attempting to adjust to the impact that managed care has on the delivery of psychological services. New areas of practice and new forms of treatment will continue to emerge as psychologists struggle to survive. However, this article focuses on the problems of the profession itself. Solutions are suggested. *[Article copies available for a fee from The Haworth Document Delivery Service: 1-800-342-9678. E-mail address: getinfo@haworthpressinc.com <Website: http://www.haworthpressinc.com>]*

KEYWORDS. Managed care, independent practice, private practice

When I received my doctoral degree in 1953, many states still did not license or certify psychologists. In most clinical settings psychologists could only test. They could not make a diagnosis. They would present their findings to the physician who would make a diagnosis. Private practicing psychologists were few in number. The big debate was whether practicing psychologists could or should do psychotherapy. There was no third party reimbursement for services provided by a psychologist.

A. Eugene Shapiro is Associate Dean and Professor, Nova Southeastern University, Ft. Lauderdale, FL.

Address correspondence to: A. Eugene Shapiro, PhD, Center for Psychological Studies, Nova Southeastern University, 3301 College Avenue, Ft. Lauderdale, FL 33314.

[Haworth co-indexing entry note]: "Professional Problems and Solutions in the Managed Care Era." Shapiro, A. Eugene. Co-published simultaneously in *Critical Strategies: Psychotherapy in Managed Care* (The Haworth Press, Inc.) Vol. 1, No. 1, 2000, pp. 39-46; and: *Psycho-Economics: Managed Care in Mental Health in the New Millennium* (ed: Robert D. Weitz) The Haworth Press, Inc., 2000, pp. 39-46. Single or multiple copies of this article are available for a fee from The Haworth Document Delivery Service [1-800-342-9678, 9:00 a.m. - 5:00 p.m. (EST). E-mail address: getinfo@haworthpressinc.com].

It wasn't until 1968, that New Jersey passed the first legislative initiative that mandated third party reimbursement for the services of a licensed psychologist for covered conditions. I believe that this act was instrumental in making private practice for psychologists a viable profession. It took several more years before almost all states passed similar legislation. At this point many of us believed that *independent practice had truly become independent.*

Unfortunately, the resolution of the independent practitioner's problems turned out to be a short lived fantasy. The arrival of managed care, with its assets and its shortcomings, became the reality. The practitioners of psychology, and all health related professions, have had to face many new and serious problems. Society has been moved from the meaningful "Doctor-Patient" relationship to the commercial "Provider-Consumer" relationship. In addition, managed care's goal is to control health care by structuring services as clearly defined, easily duplicated, interventions. Thus, if a consumer (patient) manifests certain presenting problems, the provider may only utilize approved assessment procedures, and once a diagnosis is made, employ a hierarchy of approved protocols of interventions. Since often these protocols have been developed by physicians (and pharmaceutical houses), at the top of the hierarchy is a round of medical interventions before psychotherapy can be employed. Finally, if psychotherapy is approved, the number of visits are extremely limited. In order to comply with the imposed restrictions, psychological interventions are focused on the patient's behavior and the goal is behavior modifications. *This results in a relatively simplistic view of the patient problems that most practitioners encounter.*

There are several problems that need to be addressed. One major concern is whether or not the Managed Care movement is here to stay. There are those who speak boldly about defeating this movement and returning to the good old days. However, I don't believe that is going to happen. The days of "doctor knows best" are gone. The increased costs of health care make it necessary to develop a more cost efficient system and to some extent Managed Care has accomplished that goal. Unfortunately, this is often at the expense of patient care. The major purchasers of HMO plans are corporations that provide health benefits to their employees, and State and Federal Governments in order to provide Medicaid and Medicare services. These organizations, in spite of lip service to the contrary, have essentially abrogated any responsibility to provide quality care. The driving force is not the insured's health, but the bottom line. Hospitals and doctors are employed, or efficiently managed, by the large Health Care Organizations. I read recently that this year was the first time that there were more physicians employed than there were in private practice. The dreaded clinics of yesteryear (and today in many areas), where nameless patients were treated by overworked interns and technicians, have returned. We rarely go to a physician who knows our name, or anything about us. The best assurance one has of receiving a minimum standard of care is the provider's (Hospital, Physician, Psychologist) concern about a malpractice suit. And it will only get worse.

A recent report in the *NY Times* and in *Business Week* stated that Health Maintenance Organizations are feeling the pinch between state and federal legislation that stipulate a certain minimum of care (i.e., mandatory mamograms, a 2 day hospital stay after child birth, etc.) and a narrowing margin of profit. As HMOs go head to head with other HMOs for business, they have to price themselves competitively. To accomplish this, since most of the fat has gone out of the system, quicker, cheaper, procedures employed by cheaper, less qualified professionals will be utilized. Nurses, physician assistants, and other support staff will supplant much of the physician's work. Master level technicians, under a variety of labels, will provide much of what the licensed psychologist does at lower cost.

The October 27, 1997 issue of *Business Week* ran an article entitled, "HMOs Get Hit Where it Hurts." The teaser for this story reads: "With managed care a commodity business, insurers are stuck with razor-thin margins that are getting thinner." This report details the declining profit margins in managed care organizations, the increasing clout of providers in the marketplace, the trend toward direct negotiations between group purchasers of health care and integrated systems of care, and the commoditazation of managed care in general. "What is most ironic about this trend is that managed care is now experiencing exactly what happened to health care providers with the industrialization of health care: one's services have become an off-the-shelf commodity, with price the only bargaining issue."

In spite of having licensing protection in every state, we have difficulty defining and controlling what is exclusively psychology. We control the title, i.e., who might call oneself a psychologist, however, we cannot control who does what. To the general public, all we do is talk and listen, *and a lot of people do that. The clergy has been doing it for many years,* long before there were psychologists. We do have some testing which we have jealously guarded as our own, i.e., projective testing. However, the field is disavowing these instruments which rely primarily on clinical skills. Instead, we are moving toward the increased use of paper and pencil tests, which have the advantage of being easy to administer, easy to score, the results are easily computer generated and the report can be printed without input from the psychologist. In fact, these instruments are so user-friendly that almost anyone with a modicum of training can administer them.

Psychotherapy, which we fought to make part of the psychologist's armamentarium, is no longer the exclusive domain of Psychiatrists, Licensed Psychologists, and Licensed Clinical Social Workers. Today, there is a laundry list of Bachelor's and Master's degree psychotherapists/counselors, who provide mental health care to those in need of psychological services. Sadly, some drug and alcohol counselors have as their primary credential the fact that they are recovering alcoholics or drug abusers. I recently learned that Hawaii is in the process of passing legislation that permits *non-licensed* mental health personnel to practice psychotherapy provided they do not hold themselves out as psychologists, and do not say that they are licensed to practice psychotherapy.

A lack of specificity pertains to the term *"psychotherapy."* *Psychotherapy apparently describes <u>any</u> interaction between someone <u>professing</u> to be a psychotherapist, and a client seeking help for a problem in living.* Therefore, individuals with decreasing amounts of education and training are becoming psychotherapists. And as we move increasingly toward a formulary of protocols for treatment of specific symptoms, i.e., therapy by the numbers, we make at easier for lesser trained individuals to become providers of mental health services.

It is depressing to see professional gains that were achieved over a long period of time, over medical and often corporate opposition, being eroded by encroaching managed care, and the scramble of disenfranchised health providers, including medicine, to fight to protect their domains. Psychology has a history of overcoming external conditions and forging ahead. Over the opposition of organized medicine we achieved licensing, the right to diagnose, the right to be expert witnesses, to independently provide clinical services, to be reimbursed by third parties for most clinical services rendered., and to be admitted to hospital staffs. In spite of medicine's road blocks, and the previously noted difficulties in defining ourselves in exclusive terms, psychology and psychologists have flourished, *until recently*.

The depressing headline of the July/August issue of *The National Psychologist: SURVEY: PSYCHOLOGISTS' INCOMES PLUMMET* was not terribly unexpected. The article reports that since the last survey, conducted by them in late 1995, some 30 months ago, the average annual income shrank from $86,200 to $73,850. A decrease of over 14% in 30 months. Much of the blame was attributed to the practices of managed care. The article notes "A decline from $85 per therapy hour to $60-$65 has become familiar in this health care climate."

The *My Opinion Column*, authored by Dr. Stan Lipsitz, in the July 1998 *Monitor* focuses on the downsizing of clinical psychology. After Dr. Lipsitz presents some of the consequences of downsizing, if not in number, certainly in income, he mentions pending legislative endeavors at the State and Federal level that might offer some hope. He concludes ". . . we each are left, to a greater or lesser extent, with disappointments with our professional dreams and left to find our own individual solutions. Perhaps the greatest disappointment is that no one else has the answers for us–or for our profession." *I disagree, there are answers.*

I personally believe that there is no current problem that cannot be resolved. As a profession we are better organized, more affluent and politically sophisticated than ever before. However, changes have to take place *within the profession* before we can battle fully and effectively the forces of managed care. Those of us who choose to battle the establishment have to be reconciled to the laments and complaints, not only from external forces, but often from some of our colleagues as well.

Over the years as I have involved myself in psychology's issue I am often reminded of Machiavelli as quoted in "The Prince" (1513):

> And it ought to be remembered that there is nothing more difficult to take in hand, more perilous to conduct, or more uncertain in its success, than to take the lead in the introduction of a new order of things. Because the innovator has for enemies all those who have done well under the old conditions, and luke warm defenders in those who may do well under the new. This coolness

arises partly from fear of the opponents who have the laws on their side, and partly from the incredulity of men, who do not readily believe in new things until they have long experience with them. Thus, it happens that whenever those who are hostile have the opportunity to attack they do it like partisans, whilst others defend lukewarmly. The reformer has enemies in all those who would profit from the old order and only lukewarm defenders in all those who would profit from the new order.

Having expressed my caveats, let me indicate what has to be done. Some areas will develop naturally. Psychological services will expand as we move into special areas of expertise to serve society's needs, such as neuropsychology, health psychology, and forensic to name a few. However, I have selected three areas I deem necessary of *active* support in order to structure the *uniqueness and importance* of our profession and to *promote its public image.*

For one, I call your attention to the article I wrote with Jack G. Wiggins, published in the March 1994 *American Psychologist* entitled "The PsyD for all Practicing Psychologists." We wrote the article because we noted that psychology is the only health care profession that does not have a degree that identifies who we are. A PhD (or EdD,) says nothing meaningful regarding our profession. A PhD designates any learned professional who has done a dissertation. For example, a popular radio personality who refers to herself as Dr. _____, and who dispenses all types of psychological suggestions to call-in listeners does not have a doctorate in psychology. However, she seems content to permit the public to infer that she is a psychologist. I recall seeing a calling card of a mental health counselor, who had a PhD in English, happily use the doctor degree to infer that she was a psychologist. I had a licensed social worker friend who never corrected anyone if they called him a psychologist. *OF COURSE NOT,* a psychologist is the desired profession. Recently, a friend referred to her daughter as a psychologist, when I asked where she received her doctorate, it turned out that she had an MA in Marriage and Family. The mother replied, "she is just like a psychologist."

Colleagues, I believe firmly, that you can't sell a product without a brand name. Industry knows that well and pays a lot of money for the goodwill a brand name brings. We are in the fortunate position that psychology and psychologists have excellent public recognition.

However, as a profession we have done little to exploit it. The PsyD, as a proprietary degree, and then properly advertised and marketed will help psychologists to become recognized rightfully as the best trained mental health specialists in the world. In the article, Wiggins and I spelled out how the PsyD could be awarded to appropriately trained, experienced, licensed PhD practicing psychologists through a credential review. These psychologists would hold *both* the PhD and the PsyD degrees, similar to the MD who also holds a PhD. Somewhat naively, we had hoped that an article in the *American Psychologist* would start the ball rolling. In my fantasy I imagined that psychologists would recognize the importance of our premise and would start the momentum necessary to accomplish the goal. However, in various polls taken at the division level, the PsyD was not a high priority. People were honored to hold the PhD, and many believed that having a PsyD as well as the PhD somehow diminished the PhD. Therefore the issue remains unresolved and the need for a unifying, publicly recognized degree still exists.

Another area to consider is making the *internship post doctoral*, like every other doctoral health profession. The only reason it is not postdoctoral is because in prior years there was little-to-no clinical training offered in graduate school. The internship was the place where clinical experience was attained. To maintain control over the student while on internship, and to exercise oversight of the internship, the degree was not awarded until an internship was completed satisfactorily. However, the psychological intern was at a distinct disadvantage in the health care hierarchy. All the other health care interns were "Doctors." Psychologists were Mr. or Ms. Having the internship predoctoral today makes no sense. Most of our students graduate with from 1500 to 2000 hours of supervised practicum experience. I suggest for a student to receive his or her doctoral degree prior to internship, he or she must demonstrate a minimum of 1500-2000 hours of supervised practicum experience and acceptance into an internship acceptable to their degree granting school or university. That accomplished, our doctoral level psychological interns would be on an equal footing with the other health care interns and our psychologists in training would not be viewed as lesser than other professionals. This can only help their professional self-concept. In addition, if provisional licensing could be accomplished, as it has in Florida, the internship site could possibly bill third party payers for the intern's services.

And lastly, in a more difficult arena, work must continue on authorizing specially trained psychologists to prescribe medications. While no dramatic results have occurred to date some very encouraging legislative progress can be reported. Louisiana barely missed passage of their bill last year. California has been making progress in moving their bill through the system. Several states are developing training programs and legislative initiatives. In the not too distant future we will attain the goal of prescriptive authority, if we have the *will and the leadership to make it happen.*

I have faith in the future of psychology. I'm sure that we are graduating the best and the brightest. These psychologists will be the future leaders we need. However, if we don't make the public aware of the quality of training of the "Doctor of Psychology," and if we don't enhance the public image of psychologists, and if we don't improve the self-concept of psychologists in training, the best trained mental health professionals will be relegated to dependency on the dictates of Managed Care Organizations. The only other option will be to rely solely on treating individuals who can afford private care. Sadly, our contribution to society will be diminished.

Psychological Practice, Psychotherapy and Managed Care: A Case Study

Ronald E. Fox, PhD
Ken Lessler, PhD
Charles Cooper, PhD

SUMMARY. Using one practice whose history parallels the history of independent psychological practice in the U.S. as a case example, the article chronicles the major changes in practice patterns that have occurred in response to changes in reimbursement. It attempts to show how changes in reimbursement practices have altered and shaped the scope of professional practice as well as the nature of psychological care that is available to society. It is felt that the case example has heuristic value for understanding and documenting what is happening to the profession and where it may be going. *[Article copies available for a fee from The Haworth Document Delivery Service: 1-800-342-9678. E-mail address: getinfo@haworthpressinc.com <Website: http://www.haworthpressinc.com>]*

KEYWORDS. Managed care, independent practice, private practice, psychotherapy

---

Ronald E. Fox, Ken Lessler, and Charles Cooper are affiliated with Human Resource Consultants, Chapel Hill, NC.

Address correspondence to: Ronald E. Fox, Human Resource Consultants, P.A., 104 South Estes Drive, Suite 301, Chapel Hill, NC 27514.

The authors are deeply indebted to Anne Arberg for her editorial advice and assistance in the preparation of this paper.

[Haworth co-indexing entry note]: "Psychological Practice, Psychotherapy and Managed Care: A Case Study." Fox, Ronald E., Ken Lessler, and Charles Cooper. Co-published simultaneously in *Critical Strategies: Psychotherapy in Managed Care* (The Haworth Press, Inc.) Vol. 1, No. 1, 2000, pp. 47-59; and: *Psycho-Economics: Managed Care in Mental Health in the New Millennium* (ed: Robert D. Weitz) The Haworth Press, Inc., 2000, pp. 47-59. Single or multiple copies of this article are available for a fee from The Haworth Document Delivery Service [1-800-342-9678, 9:00 a.m. - 5:00 p.m. (EST). E-mail address: getinfo@haworthpressinc.com].

47

In less than a decade, the movement of third party reimbursement from a primarily indemnity insurance system to one in which benefits are managed or controlled has drastically reduced both the payments for psychotherapeutic treatment and the incomes of psychologists and other mental health professionals who provide such services. The effect of managed care on the availability and delivery of psychotherapeutic services in the U.S. is best understood in the context of the growth and development of psychological practice over the past four decades. In a brief time period that can be encompassed in a single professional career, reimbursement for psychological psychotherapy has moved from a situation in which there was no third party reimbursement for psychologists providing psychotherapy independently, through a period in which most plans recognized psychologists, and finally to the current situation in which psychologists are recognized providers, but psychotherapeutic treatment is a covered expense only when it is administered in increasingly low dosages by those willing to accept a lower reimbursement rate and who are typically less well trained. Psychologists may have won the battle to be recognized as providers on a par with psychiatrists, while losing the war to preserve the management of that care, the ability to fully charge for the service, and ultimately perhaps, the opportunity to provide the service.

Using one practice whose history parallels the history of independent psychological practice in the U.S. as a case example, the following article chronicles the major changes in practice patterns that have occurred in response to changes in reimbursement. We will show how changes in reimbursement and management practices have altered and shaped the scope of professional practice as well as the nature of the psychological care that is available to society. While we make no claim that the practice in the case example is representative of all types of psychological practice in all parts of the country, we do believe that it is representative of many of them, and therefore has heuristic value for understanding and documenting what is happening to our profession and where it may be going.

IN THE BEGINNING: THE 1960s

The practice was founded by a psychologist in the mid-1960s near the time that the state's first psychological licensing law was enacted. He was arguably the first psychologist to enter full-time, independent practice in the state, followed slowly at first by a small handful of others. At that time, non-physicians were not recognized as qualified independent mental health providers for insurance reimbursement. The few indemnity plans which did cover treatment for mental illnesses restricted coverage to services provided by physicians. A freedom of choice law prohibiting insurers from discriminating against properly credentialed psychologists did not come into being in the state until several years later. Although he was well-trained as a psychotherapist, and was a diplomate in clinical psychology, he was able to attract only a few upper middle-class patients who could afford his fees without insurance coverage. Consequently, he built his practice primarily by providing a broad range of assessment, education, consultation, and research and evaluation services to a variety of programs which were heavily supported by federal and state governments. Juvenile justice diversion programs, Head Start, and various early childhood screening projects were only a few of those that were available. As administrators became familiar with his capabilities and learned what psychologists were able to provide, practice opportunities expanded. New members were recruited to the practice to help meet the rising demand. The recruits included psychologists, teachers, and speech therapists, with pediatricians, public health experts, and psychology professors working on the consulting staff. Within the space of 5 years, what began as a solo practice had grown to include 2 full-time practitioners and 6 part-time consultants supported by 2 full-time staff members.

The beginning years had several effects on the way the practice developed which should be noted:

- Psychotherapy was the preferred professional activity of both the founder and the colleagues who joined him;
- However, psychotherapy was only one of several distinct professional services offered by the group.
- Psychotherapy was viewed as the "Cadillac" of professional services, offering, as it did, a prestigious professional goal and an appropriate forum in which to practice hard-earned skills. It had the intellectual and professional cache absent from such activities as consulting with a Head Start program in a rural part of the state. Unlike many other psychological services, psychotherapy could be done in the psychologist's office. Responsibility for payment for psychotherapy was easier to pinpoint than services

delivered to governmental agencies. Contracting with patients seemed easier, more convenient and more certain than the constant, unseemly scramble for public funds. Finally, filling one's schedule with a steady stream of private patients offered far more control of one's time and income than operating within the strictures of the competing needs and demands of the numerous individuals involved in other types of services.

- Psychotherapy was a service offered mainly to the "carriage trade," and was paid for primarily out of personal, private funds.
- An embryonic "de facto" two-tiered system of care started to emerge in which those with money or insurance were treated by the most qualified and experienced members of the profession, while those without such means were treated by less experienced professionals and supported by publicly supported grants and contracts. It should be noted that the growth in private practice occurred concurrently with the growth of public funding for community health services.
- At that time, the struggle for recognition as psychotherapists on a par with psychiatrists seemed to be more about a struggle for status and prestige than about the money that would come along.
- The majority of the services which provided the bulk of the psychologists' income during the early period of the practice were supported by public funds.

THE GOLDEN YEARS: THE 1970s AND 80s

Freedom-of-choice legislation and increasingly sophisticated pressure by professional associations gradually led to the full recognition of psychologists as qualified independent providers of psychotherapeutic services for patients whose health insurance provided mental health benefits. Furthermore, there was a marked increase in the number of health plans which were including mental illness as a covered condition. These changes brought psychotherapy to the majority of the working middle-class and a host of new opportunities for psychologists to treat them. During this period, the practice grew steadily from 2 full-time providers in 1970 to 12 in 1985, plus 5 support staff personnel. It consisted of psychologists and members of other recognized professions.

A pattern of practice growth and development was established for most of those who joined the practice: veteran practitioners filled their time with private psychotherapy patients with good insurance coverage, while turning over less lucrative and less prestigious forms of services to newly recruited, younger providers. Consultation, assessment, program evaluation, and many other services were viewed as temporary ways for new members of the group to support themselves until they could build a "real" (i.e., psychotherapy) practice. Of course, the provision of non-psychotherapeutic services also served to keep the practice in the public eye while increasing contacts for psychotherapy case-finding.

Well before what we are calling the golden years, public pressure was building to pare or reduce governmental programs in response to increased foreign competition and a soaring national debt. Eventually, the downward pressure led to drastic reductions or elimination of many of the public programs that previously had supported a number of services offered by the practice. As outside funding declined, the group's providers restricted their practices more and more to psychotherapy. For most of them, the choice was an easy one. Patients were plentiful, the pay was good, and the uncertainty of public support with its shifting priorities and constantly changing requirements was removed. The gradual disappearance of many publicly supported programs meant that newly trained psychologists brought into the practice now had to support themselves primarily through psychotherapeutic treatment.

The complexion of the practice also began to change. In initial years there were research meetings, project meetings, training of young staff for consultation practice, the production of published and unpublished papers, and the development of special services for the diagnosis and treatment of educational problems in children. This pattern contrasts sharply with the next phase in which there was an emphasis on increasing individual and group therapy skills through outside training, internal seminars and a supervision program for young psychologists that was both extensive and intensive in scope. The practice now looked very different in terms of day-to-day operations. There was less work done as a team and more done in the privacy of the consulting room.

Some implications of these developments for professional psychology and psychotherapy include the following:

- Eventually the convenience and higher fees that came with insurance reimbursement, the increased internal and external staff required for other programs, and the reduction of public funding for them, led to an over-emphasis on psychotherapy and to the virtual abandonment of other viable, alternative types of service as a part of psychological care, delivered by independent practitioners.
- Independent practitioners tended to be the most experienced members of the profession. They both provided the models and set the standards for practice in the community.
- Community clinics and other publicly funded programs could neither attract nor retain experienced practitioners in the face of the competition provided by third-party reimbursement. They were also hindered by the increasing demands of the positions and the fact that they served a population with whom psychologists identified less easily.
- Over time, insurance money supplanted public funding for the psychotherapy provided by independent practitioners.
- Generations of practitioners were produced who believed that the practice of psychology consisted solely–or at least most gloriously–of providing psychotherapeutic services. Many of the consultative, evaluation, assessment, research, prevention, outreach and wellness services provided by the original practitioners had fallen into such disuse that they were not commonly a part of graduate practicum educational experiences and certainly were no longer viewed as viable, or even desirable, sources of the kind of income as that provided by doing psychotherapy.
- Because private practitioners came to be dependent on psychotherapy as their sole source of income, they were poorly prepared and positioned for either anticipating or dealing with the radical changes occasioned by changes in the market place: the management of health care expenditures by businesses in order to reduce spiraling personnel costs. Younger psychologists in the practice no longer had a broad survival and entrepreneurial view of practice which would have helped insure their survival and thus, they were poorly positioned to weather the impending major shifts in practice demands.

THE ERA OF MANAGED CARE:
THE LATE 1980s TO THE MID 1990s

In 1986 the practice agreed to work with a managed care firm to develop a managed mental health delivery system that would reduce the number of hospital admissions and the length of hospital stays while maintaining quality of care. The group entered the agreement hoping it might insure the role of psychology in this new approach to health care. By that time, the group had a thriving practice in two well-established sites with services dispensed by 15 clinicians and six support staff.

For the practice, the managed care agreement marked the beginning of the most rapid change in the region's health care market that had ever been seen, and it also initiated a period of internal dissent not experienced previously. Initially, the practice was highly effective in helping to reduce inpatient treatment costs by offering emergency and various other alternative treatment services. The practice flourished: collaborative relationships with primary care providers were enhanced, cooperative ventures with inpatient psychiatrists were established, patients received better, more integrated care, high standards of care were maintained, conflicts-of-interest concerns of providers where easily managed, and the employers who contracted with the managed care firm were saving money.

Others did not approve of the changes. They conducted meetings in which psychologists, assisted by members of the university philosophy department, hotly debated the ethics of a practice in which profits were being increased as care was being decreased. In addition to the ethical dilemmas, the practice also was forced to deal with high-paid providers of long-term care who resented or ignored the review and management of care required by the new system, no matter how benign its stated intent. In an effort to avoid a schism which threatened to tear the practice apart, a number of new providers were contracted to work as professional employees of the practice for a fixed and invariably reduced fee thus removing them from a conflict of interest. The new recruits, more often than not, were beginning professionals or persons whose interest was in supplementing their income.

Dissension from within was not the only stress that came with the new economy. There was an increased sense of backlash and suspiciousness from other practices as well. Because of its size, the practice was frequently seen by smaller practices as a threat to their fair market share. New practices or innovations proposed by a group that was by then one of the largest in the southeastern U.S. were viewed by others as simple marketing ploys to divert and capture the available clientele. Relationships of any kind that were established with a managed care company were seen both as efforts to exclude competitors and as confirming evidence that the group was bargaining with the devil.

Clearly, the changes noted did not represent the best of times. Yet, even amid the unrest, some of the changes that resulted were good for the practice! Closer working relationships formed with primary care physicians resulted in better, more integrated care for many patients. Taking a good hard look at the effectiveness of our treatment and becoming more discriminating in dispensing long-term psychotherapy both saved money and led to more appropriate care for patients. A system was developed to provide more efficient and convenient continuum of care. Finally, a number of special services were developed to meet the needs of some special populations. These services would not have been put in place without the pressures created by the new managed care market. In many ways, it was an exciting and trying time for both factions of the practice. For a few, the changes gave those with the vision to see it an opportunity to manage themselves while also providing high quality care in the challenging environment of capitated care. They reacted positively to the opportunity of doing good for others, while reducing costs and preserving their own incomes. For others, the challenge and excitement came from the identification and reaffirmation of deeply held values and the hope of preserving a human service that is greatly needed to help.

For a brief time, all seemed well despite a sense of underlying turbulence. In other parts of the country, psychologists were uniting in endeavors similar to ones created by our own group. Partnerships between psychologists and business people were developing which would have been unheard of only a few years earlier. A national coalition of psychologists to work in concert with business to reduce costs was proposed. At the state level proposed efforts to cope with the new situation was to form a provider PPO which would provide some stability in a world of frenzied mergers, take-overs, and buy-outs.

Briefly, it seemed that the tide had been stemmed, that the worst was over. Soon, however, the pressures to save more money, reduce health care costs even further, and increase the already bloated profits of the entrepreneurs who now owned the health care system, led to the rapid corporatization of the health care industry. In the space of a few years, the critical decisions regarding health care services moved from the hands of practitioners to those of case managers. The temple of health was now in the hands of the money lenders.

The move from self-management to management by external case managers created effects as extensive as they were dramatic. Every practitioner–veterans and neophytes, psychologists, social workers, psychiatrists, nurses, and counselors alike–felt the effects of the change. Incomes dropped while overhead was going through the roof. The work load of office staff was increased substantially at a time when funds to expand their numbers were not available. Practice patterns were changed and molded by new realities. Like hospitalization, long-term outpatient care all but disappeared as a treatment option. Almost overnight, short-term psychotherapy and medication became the only treatments approved for reimbursement. All the energy appeared to be focused on reducing costs and saving money. Almost no attention was paid to improving service. "Treatment plans," "prior authorization," "retrospective reviews," "medical necessity," "case managers," "provider panels," "HMOs," "closed panels," "preferred provider groups," and a host of other unfamiliar terms entered the group's lexicon.

Incredibly, managed care companies then found a way to make the situation even more onerous. In addition to slashed costs and severely restricted care, they handed back the old ethical issues in the form of "case rates." Case rates placed the practice on the old seesaw of decreasing reimbursement in the face of increased need for service by less healthy patient populations. Additionally, more service and treatment responsibility was now required to obtain the managed care contract and remain in business; but less funds were available to provide what was being demanded. This time the issue was not one of profit or less profit, but one of loss or more loss! An analysis of costs revealed that the overhead expenses associated with patients on a case rate basis was 6 to 7 times more expensive than the overhead for patients covered by indemnity insurance! Providers who believed more care was necessary after the half dozen visits that were actually funded under such contracts, were faced with patients whose contracts called for up to twenty or twenty-four visits. Once again ethical concerns became a regular agenda item at practice management meetings.

LATE 1990s: WHERE NEXT

In an effort to provide as much care as possible with fewer and fewer dollars, the practice developed more specialized group and individual programs: brief solutions clinic, focused problem clinic, self-esteem program, emergency care services, and the like. Simultaneously, efforts were mounted to increase the dollars coming into the practice via other avenues. Some services (such as Employee Assistance Programs) which had been staples of the practice for many years were expanded and marketed aggressively to employers, yielding new business and often leading to spin-off services. Several practitioners developed specialized niches in such areas as sex therapy, health psychology, brief assessment techniques, career counseling, two-career families, stress management and various consultation services to businesses and organizations.

The changes noted were made in response to unprecedented and unanticipated economic pressures. Further, the changes themselves were far from being merely cosmetic. By the end of the current decade, the very warp and woof of the fabric of mental health care in the US will have been changed. That is a fact. Yet, after all the changes, our practice has come full circle, leaving us where we began but with different entities responsible for paying the bills. Once again, psychotherapy of clinically determined length is available primarily only to the affluent. Similar conditions exist for some highly specialized treatments such as sex therapy. Brief, problem-oriented, highly focused and specialized clinical services, or medication are the only services available to the majority of our patients these days. These are generalizations, to be sure. But, in the main, the fact of the matter is that the current health care economy has reinforced a two-tiered system of care in which the distinction between the haves and the have-nots grows greater by the day.

Managed care has helped foster a number of low-cost services that are much needed. Many of them are ones that existed years ago in community mental health centers and were supported by public funds. Those funds have dwindled, and now private moneys have given new life to preventive and crises services in order to save money. Private moneys are providing support, minimal though it may be, for services that were funded by public programs in the 1960s. Our practice group has been expended in order to provide some of the services which payers now expect us to provide. Presently, there are 24 clinicians and 7.5 support staff.

In some respects, the nature of our practice group resembles what was it was like 30 years ago, with several critical differences. Open-ended, restorative psychotherapy is still regarded as the highest and best level of care and once again it is available, for the most part, only to the affluent. As before, such treatment is provided primarily by the most experienced and most highly trained members of the profession who have developed reputations and contacts over many years. However, less and less of this care is being paid for by the kinds of indemnity insurance plans that were common only two decades ago. Increasingly, the patients themselves pay for such care. Other forms of care, which are seen by many professionals as effective only for symptom relief or emergency treatment, are available for the masses and provided by lesser trained and less experienced providers. This is especially troublesome given the fact that rapid and effective crisis intervention requires the greatest amount of professional responsibility and, frequently, the highest level of skill as well. Mental health services are now provided by insurance that is administered by managed care firms. The bulk of the working middle-class patients are now unable to afford individual, restorative psychotherapy, much less the growth and self-actualization services whose preventative value is well-established. This is a very different reality. For the first time in a long time, the middle class is receiving virtually the same services as the lower socio-economic population served by the public sector. Those with money receive a higher quality of care by more qualified providers.

Several other effects on the nature of practice and our providers should be noted. Hierarchical and artificial patterns of practice have emerged in response to reimbursement practices that may not be in the long-term public interest:

- Psychiatrists receive so much more money for prescribing medications than for doing psychotherapy that almost none of them do anything else. In fact, many managed care companies limit access to psychotherapy provided by psychiatrists. The result is that psychotherapy is underutilized, medications are over-utilized, and fewer providers are taking the time to really listen to their patients. This is certainly a loss to the large number of psychiatrists who spent much of their professional life learning to be therapists. Many psychiatry programs today give only cursory attention to therapy.

- Older, presumably wiser and more competent practitioners are seeing the "carriage trade" for more money than their younger colleagues can command and the gap between the two is widening. Even in the early days of managed care, the compensation for psychotherapy was sufficient for veteran practitioners in a large practice to share some higher fee cases with junior colleagues and then fill the resulting gaps in their own schedules with "lower fee" cases. That is no longer possible. Insurance plans which less than 10 years ago were paying $90 per session, may now pay only $35–a sum which creates rather than fills gaps.

- In the current market, there are few incentives to obtain highly specialized training. Most new cases are shunted to generalists and the least expensive (and thus less well-trained) providers. The incentive in today's market is to be a member of a large provider network with many service contracts with the goal of insuring survival as a practitioner. For many professionals, even low pay is better than none. Those who are not on the right panels or in the winning networks get nothing as more and more covered lives are pulled into the managed care arena. They are not in the game and at risk of not being able to remain in practice.

The current system changes the motivations and distorts the career paths of those who are drawn to the field. In today's market, a new psychologist joining the practice cannot count on being able to earn an income sufficient to raise and support a family for many years. Gone is the time when junior colleagues gained valuable experiences by serving lower fee patients while having enough regular fee clients to earn a livable wage. In an era in which almost everyone is a low fee patient, the incentives change. New providers now learn to move as quickly as possible into a market niche in which they can provide services for the more well-to-do. The lesser pay patients are no longer sources of valuable experience, they are stepping stones to a decent income. The link between social need and practitioner incentives has been shattered. Sooner or later, it must be re-forged.

CONCLUDING COMMENTS

The jury is out regarding the enduring changes that will remain as the health care market continues to evolve. The practice is struggling to retain supposedly secure, but very low income from various HMO and managed care companies while changing other parts of itself into self-pay or direct organizational pay services. The alternatives are beginning to work but no one really knows what the long term effects of the radical changes that have taken place will be on psychological practice. Some, ever in the role of explorers and visionaries, continue to attempt new and different organizational structures with different combinations of players which are intended to regain control of the mental health dollar and how it is spent. A lot has happened to transform psychotherapy from one of the last cottage industries into a commodity dispensed by corporate moguls. Much more change lies ahead. While no one can read the future, psychotherapy still remains a valued product and psychologists still are better trained to dispense it than any other profession. It would be premature to write an obituary for psychological psychotherapy. We have reached the end of another chapter, not the end of the book. The practice, founded over three decades ago, worked well for another time and place. The one that has evolved seems to be working well in a very different set of circumstances. What the future holds is unclear, but we do intend to be a part of it–to be delivering needed, quality care to a society that is much in need of it. If history is any predictor of the future, we believe that psychology (and our practice) will do much better than simply survive. We believe that it also will be possible to thrive.

Mastering the Technology of Change

Lisa B. Freudenberger, CAC, PhD
Herbert J. Freudenberger, PhD
Dorothy Sharlip, MSW

SUMMARY. In the newly changed managed care environment, psychologists can distinguish themselves both as scientists and practitioners. Psychologists have been working steadily to quantify their offerings. Researchers have not only confirmed the efficacy and effectiveness of psychotherapy, they have been studying specific in-session and out-of-session factors that will help predict when, how, and with whom, to provide which psychological services. Our knowledge of all that precedes treatment and all that is required to maintain treatment gains will help us market ourselves with more authority. Our ability to create services based on this knowledge will become our most valued offering to the payor driven medical establishment and the underwriters of medical care. *[Article copies available for a fee from The Haworth Document Delivery Service: 1-800-342-9678. E-mail address: getinfo@haworthpressinc.com <Website: http://www.haworthpressinc.com>]*

KEYWORDS. Managed care, psychotherapy, independent practice, private practice

We approach the millennium as we do the stairmaster. The technology of change is available. Will we take the necessary steps to assure our professional health? When will we begin? How long will it take?

Lisa B. Freudenberger is in Private Practice, New York, NY.
Herbert J. Freudenberger is in Private Practice, New York, NY.
Dorothy Sharlip is in Private Practice, Long Island, NY.

[Haworth co-indexing entry note]: "Mastering the Technology of Change." Freudenbeger, Lisa B., Herbert J. Freudenberger, and Dorothy Sharlip. Co-published simultaneously in *Critical Strategies: Psychotherapy in Managed Care* (The Haworth Press, Inc.) Vol. 1, No. 1, 2000, pp. 61-70; and: *Psycho-Economics: Managed Care in Mental Health in the New Millennium* (ed: Robert D. Weitz) The Haworth Press, Inc., 2000, pp. 61-70. Single or multiple copies of this article are available for a fee from The Haworth Document Delivery Service [1-800-342-9678, 9:00 a.m. - 5:00 p.m. (EST). E-mail address: getinfo@haworthpressinc.com].

As psychologists and providers of behavioral health care services, we need to encourage ourselves to find new ways to incorporate our knowledge into the work we do. We can utilize our research findings to enhance our work and to secure our place in the future.

The business of medicine has impacted steadily on behavioral health care. Last to board the runaway train of medical money making and first to be "carved out" and pared down, we have been forced to evaluate the quality and quantity of the services we provide. Despite our initial tendency toward resistance, we've learned a great deal. We will be wise to embrace opportunities for new development with optimism and discipline.

Let's take a moment to follow this trend. HMOs, most notably Kaiser Permanente and Harvard Community Health Plan, were among the first to inspire creativity and camaraderie around mental health care resource allocation. Having demonstrated the ability to contain costs and to offer high quality mental health services to their enrollees, they served as models for further experimentation as mental health care benefits changed.

Capitated benefits began to replace rich indemnity coverage for those insured Americans who accessed mental health services. At the very least, lucrative contracts for administrative services only were being offered in an effort to study ways to contain costs. Despite the fact that benefits were made available to larger numbers of insured workers, the percentage of total health care costs spent for behavioral health was reduced from 6.1 in 1998 to 3.1 in 1997 (Jensen et al., 1998). Entrepreneurs were able to profit substantially with aggressive utilization management based on gerry-rigged standards for medical necessity.

Medical necessity became the focus of a tug-of-war between managed care companies and practitioners. Those who had been passionate about getting patients into treatment and keeping them there to help them grow were being forced to rethink this standard.

Changes occurred on many fronts. In-patient facilities were closed, beds were limited and intermediate levels of care were created to assure resource conservation. Abuses of over-utilization of services were dealt with harshly. Long hospital stays and stable caseloads of familiar ambulatory patients were replaced by pressure to produce a type of treatment that fit faithfully into the "least restrictive" level of care. Admissions to hospitals were managed very closely with diversions to partial day programs occurring regularly. Psychotherapy was no longer automatically covered. Without pre-authorization, the therapeutic process could not begin.

The potential for burnout during this era of rapid change skyrocketed. As Herbert Freudenberger describes, many of us experienced some level of stress: "The degree to which the perceived expectation and the degree of differential rewards expected from meeting or not meeting that demand reflect the amount of stress that person experiences." Unfortunately, some met his criterion for burnout. They experienced "a feeling of progressive deterioration . . . a loss of motivation that tends . . . to . . . affect . . . attitudes, mood, and general behavior" (Freudenberger, 1998). For each of us who has attempted to adjust to the intrusions of managed care, there has been a colleague who has pointed out the pitfalls of embracing the medical model. We have been urged to drop our "having it all mentality . . . and reclaim our professional souls," and we have been reminded of the dangers of malpractice litigation (Pipal, 1995).

A large group of recipients were being offered brief symptom-focused interventions, usually when they were in crisis. "Flight into health" and "spontaneous remission" were being viewed positively. Personal growth and satisfaction with life issues, previously valued treatment goals, were considered a luxury unless proven to provide medical offset, and those data were inconclusive (Pallack et al., 1995; Simon et al., 1995; & Zimet, 1989). The safe-guards developed to protect the human rights of the most seriously mentally ill served payors well in the shortrun.

Until recently, managed care companies were able to transition seriously and persistently mentally ill patients to the safety-net of the public sector to avoid the financial risk they pose. Managing Medicare and Medicaid has provided a new level of challenge that may render managed care, as we know it, obsolete. Large hospital-based provider groups are vying for public sector contracts that eliminate the middleman and put "risk" back into the hands of the provider. As Friedman and Savage so aptly remind us in attempting to answer the question "Can Ethical Management and Managed Care Coexist?": "While it may be a challenge to remember that patients must be put ahead of profits, it is both possible and desirable to optimize the health of the patient and the organization simultaneously" (Friedman & Savage, 1998). It makes little difference whether care is managed within provider groups, themselves, or by outside organizations.

If "at risk" contracting ever shifts our focus away from our patients and onto our incomes, our ability to be fully professional will be jeopardized. Fortunately, for most of us, the potential for human tragedy is enough to keep us high-minded. For insurers, if not for providers, the fear of litigation has begun to right the balance between profitability and responsibility. PARCA legislation in Congress is just one of many examples of the political pendulum swinging back in the direction of health care entitlement now that cost-containment has been assured.

In order to qualify for contracts within the medical establishment, mental health services will be created that may seem to bear little resemblance to what practitioners (physicians included) thought they'd signed up for. Innovations such as "seamless verticalization of services" will take providers out of their specialized levels of care and back into the business of treating the same patients at every level of acuity. Except for those who limit their practices to pure psychoanalysis and will be forced to return to out-of-pocket or pro-bono financial arrangements, when criteria for medical necessity cannot be met, many of us will find ourselves practicing very much the way we did before behavioral health care became a covered benefit–if the truth were to be told. We will treat our patients when they will accept treatment with the most suitable procedures available.

Fortunately, psychologists have been working steadily to quantify their offerings. Researchers have not only confirmed the efficacy and effectiveness of psychotherapy, they have been studying specific in-session and out-of-session factors that will help predict when, and how, and with whom, to provide which psychological services.

One unusually ambitious managed care company participated in the development of an individualized patient profiling system based on a dosage and phase model of psychotherapy. Claiming to be able to predict an optimal treatment course based on Mental Health Index scores before and during treatment, this group, its case managers, and its providers were able to make treatment decisions with some objectivity (Howard et al., 1995 & 1996). The work of Howard and his colleagues provided the ballast for this endeavor and spans the better part of two decades.

Operationalizing "therapeutic effort (dosage, restrictiveness, and cumulative episode costs)" was proposed as early as 1986, by Newman and Howard as a way to inform public policy (Newman & Howard, 1986). As Newman and Tejeda so aptly summarize in their response to Seligman's provocative *Consumer Reports* Study (Seligman, 1995): "Technology now exists at such a level that we can adapt our techniques to the demands of the stakeholders in the (managed care) environment of mental health service delivery" (Newman & Tejeda, 1996). Along with their esteemed colleagues whose inspiring responses to Seligman will guide the next generation of psychotherapy research and health care policy (Barlow, 1996 & Strupp, 1996), these authors suggest that our technology is sufficient to guide program development for even the most seriously and persistently mentally ill.

DRGs and critical pathways were developed so that hospitals could maintain their economic stability while patients were assured appropriate care. Only in psychiatry have we failed, until recently, to begin to standardize treatment. The recent movement among psychiatrists and psychologists to pool their research findings and to work co-operatively will undoubtedly enhance the development of treatment protocols (Barkas et al., 1996 & Kocsis, 1996). A critical path model for treating depression that Berman et al. adapted from the Agency for Health Care Policy and Research is an excellent example of one of the ways to describe what we do and when we do it (Berman et al., 1998).

Probably the most interesting thing about what we do, however, is describing what we don't do. In drug trials, only patients who accept treatment (the drug) are included in statistical analyses of treatment effectiveness. Patients who refuse medications are not considered treatment failures; they are not counted. Our knowledge of all that precedes treatment and all that is required to maintain treatment gains will help us market ourselves with more authority. Our ability to create services based on this knowledge will become our most-valued offering to the payor driven medical establishment and the underwriters of medical care.

The cumulative work of Prochaska, DiClemente, and Norcross provides us with the tools to better predict the preferred timing for specific treatments with specific patients so as to conserve resources (Prochaska et al., 1992 & 1994). Also spanning the better part of the last two decades, the work of these researchers proposes a transtheoretical model for treatment based on stages of change. Originally funded by NIH, in an effort to understand why smoking cessation programs weren't working, Prochaska and his colleagues have identified six stages of change: Precontemplation, Contemplation, Preparation, Action, Maintenance, and Termination.They have been able to demonstrate which therapeutic processes are most helpful within each stage, and have supported the movement toward psychotherapy integration.

Patients have begun to become more educated and knowledgeable about mental health care.We conjecture that they have intuitively self-selected into insight-oriented or action-oriented psychotherapies, based on their individual stages of change. When personal growth is at stake, it may not be critical to be exacting about this selection process. With potentially life-threatening medical conditions, high-risk behaviors, or psychiatric illness, however, it is imperative that we not squander therapeutic effort on interventions that are not likely to succeed.

At least one school of psychotherapy theory has incorporated a stage of change assessment into its treatment recommendations. A cognitive technique, the motivational syllogism, has been proposed for patients presenting for treatment in the pre-contemplation stage of change. Using insights gained though Socratic questioning, patients are better able to agree to treatment goals and to prepare for action (DiGiuseppe, 1998). Its leader, Albert Ellis, leaves his appointment book with his receptionist so that his patients can decide for themselves when they are ready for their next "dose" of REBT. At the Harvard Community Health Plan it has also been customary to rely on patients to decide when to schedule their next appointments. The fact that these patients continue to be followed by primary care providers is in part a safeguard against serious disturbance continuing to go untreated (Kreilkamp, 1989).

In the world of managed care, patients who are not dangerous are not hospitalized, and patients who believe they can remain asymptomatic on medication only can be returned to primary care–at least experimentally. Instead of being threatened by these developments, why not take them as opportunities to create truly appropriate levels of care? Why not see our most troubled patients as often as it takes to keep them safe by using the time we've freed up by encouraging experimentation with independence? Why not offer our patients as well as our payors services that are not only "least restrictive" but also most likely to succeed?

In conclusion, we need to ask ourselves why it continues to be difficult for us to utilize our technology. What stage of change are *we* in? In the past, we might have wondered about our resistance and our countertransference issues. Now we can identify ways to move into the "action" stage. We need to develop services based on the technology that is available. Accurate assessment at the onset of treatment needs to occur in a different way. We need to find the best fit for the patient. For an initial therapeutic step, psychoeducation will often be offerred. As a patient gets ready for "action," additional modalities of appropriate treatment will be warranted.

Psychologists are in a unique position to become leaders in this undertaking. Psychiatrists continue to provide medical consultation and psychopharmacology. Social workers continue to provide the vast majority of psychotherapy services. Psychologists are scientist/practitioners who are schooled in the development and refinement of test administration. Psychologists are under-represented in managed care companies but can guide the development of services at the organizational level as well as for individual patients and their families. Using interventions strategically and not remaining wed to one type of treatment for all patients, we can create an excitement in our work that we can now further embrace. In the newly changed managed care environment, psychologists can distinguish themselves both as scientists and as practitioners.

REFERENCES

Barchas, J.D., Marzuk, P.M., & Beutler, L.E. (1996). Introduction to the special section on the contribution of psychotherapy and pharmacotherapy research to national mental health care. *Journal of Consulting and Clinical Psychology, 64,* 635-637.

Barlow, D.H. (1995). Health care policy, psychotherapy research, and the future of psychotherapy. *American Psychologists, 51,* 1050-1058.

Berman, W.H., Rosen, C.S., Hurt, S.W., & Kolarz, C.M. (1998). Toto, We're Not in Kansas Anymore: Measuring and Using Outcomes in Behavioral Health Care. *Clinical Psychology Science and Practice, 5,* 115-133.

Clarkin, J.F., Pilkonis, P.A., & Magruder, K.M. (1996). Psychotherapy of depression: Implications for reform of the health care system. *Archives of General Psychiatry, 53,* 717-723.

Cochrane, S.D. (1984). Preventing medical noncompliance in the outpatient treatment of bipolar affective disorders. *Journal of Consulting and Clinical Psychology, 52,* 873-878.

Cummings, N., Pallak, M., & Cummings, J. (eds). (1996). *Surviving the demise of solo practice: Mental health practitioners prospering in the era of managed care.* Madison, CT: Psychosocial Press.

DeLeon, P.H., VandenBos, G.R., & Cummings, N.A. (1983). Psychotherapy–Is it safe, effective, and appropriate? The beginning of an evoluntionary dialogue. *American Psychologist, 38,* 907-911.

DiGiuseppe, R., and Li, C.E. (1998). Treating Aggressive Children with Rational-Emotive Behavior Therapy, in *The Handbook of Psychotherapies with Children and Families*, (Eds.) Ollendick, T. and Russ, S.

Employer Expenditures for Behavioral Health Benefits Dropped 54 Percent in the Past Decade, Study Shows. *Psychiatric Services*, 49, 982-983.

Fraser, J.S. (1996). All that glitters is not always gold: Medical offset effects and managed behavioral health care. *Professional Psychology: Research and Practice*, *27*, 335-344.

Freudenberger, H.J. (1975). The staff burn-out syndrome in alternative institutions. *Psychother Theory, Res Pract 12:1.*

———. (1984a). Burnout and job dissatisfaction: Impact on the family. In *Perspectives on Work and Family*, edited by J.C. Hammer and S.H. Cramer. Rockville, MD: Aspen.

———. (1984b). Substance abuse in the work place. *Cont Drug Prob*, 11(2):245.

Freudenberger, H.J. and G. North. (1986). *Women's Burnout: How to Spot It, How to Reverse It and How to Prevent It*. New York: Penguin Books.

Freudenberger, H.J. and G. Richelson. (1981). *Burnout: How to Beat the High Cost of Success*. New York: Bantam Books.

Freudenberger, H.J. (1998). Stress and Burnout and Their Implications in the Work Environment. *Encyclopedia of Occupational Health and Safety. 5*, 15-17.

Friedman, L.H., & Savage, G.T. (1998) Can Ethical Management and Managed Care Coexist? *Health Care Management Review*, *23*, 56-62.

Garfield, S.L. (1996). Some problems associated with "validated" forms of psychotherapy. *Clincial Psychology: Science and Practice*, *3*, 218-229.

Greenberg, L.S., & Newman, F.L. (1996). An approach to psychotherapy change process research: Introduction to the special section. *Journal of Consulting and Clinical Psychology*, *64*, 435-438.

Howard, K.I., Brill, P.L., Lueger, R.J., O'Mahoney, M.T., & Grissom, G.R. (1995). *Integra outpatient tracking assessment*. Philadelphia: Compass Information Services, Inc.

Howard, K.I., Cornille, T.A., Lyons, J.S., Vessey, J.T., Lueger, R.J., & Suander, S.M. (1996). Patterns of mental health services utilization. *Archives of General Psychiatry*, *53*, 696-703.

Howard, K.I., Kopta, S.M., Krause, M.S., & Orlinsky, D.E. (1986). The dose-effect relationship in psychotherapy. *American Psychologist*, *41*, 159-164.

Howard, K.I., Lueger, R., Maling, M., & Martinovich, Z. (1993). A phase model of psychotherapy: Casual mediation of outcome. *Journal of Consulting and Clinical Psychology*, *61,* 678-685.

Howard, K.I., Moras, K., Brill, P.L., Martinovich, Z., & Lutz, W. (1996). Evaluation of psychotherapy: Efficacy effectiveness, and patient progress. *American Psychologist*, *51*, 1059-1064.

Jacobson, N.S., & Hollon, S.D. (1996a). Cognitive behavior therapy vs. pharmacotherapy: Now that the jury's returned its verdict, it's time to present the rest of the evidence. *Journal of Consulting and Clinical Psychology*, *64*, 74-80.

Jensen, G.A., Rost, K., Burton, R.P.D., & Bulycheva, Maria (1998). Mental Health

Insurance in the 1990s: Are Employers Offering Less to More? *Health Affairs, 17,* 201-208.

Kazdin, A.E. (1993a). Evaluation in clinical practice: Clinically sensitive and systematic methods of treatment delivery. *Behavior Therapy, 24,* 11-45.

Kocsis, J.H. (1996). Practice guidelines and professional challenges: What Psychotherapists need to do. *Archives of General Psychiatry, 53,* 303-304.

Kopta, S.M., Howard, K.I., Lowry, J.L., & Beutler, L.E. (1994). Patterns of symptomatic recovery in psychotherapy. *Journal of Consulting and Clinical Psychology, 62,* 1009-1016.

Luborsky, L., Diguer, L., Luborskyh, E., McLellan, A.T., Woody, G., & Alexander, L. (1993). Psychological health-sickness (pp.PHS) as a predictor of outcome in dynamic and other therapies. *Journal of Consulting and Clinical Psychology, 61,* 542-548.

Newman, F.L., & Howard, K.I. (1986). Therapeutic effort, outcome, and policy. *American Psychologist, 41,* 181-187.

Newman, F., & Tejeda, M. (1996). The need for research that is designed to support decisions in the delivery of mental health services. *American Psychologist, 51,* 1040-1049.

Norcross, J.C., & Newman, C.F. (1992). Psychotherapy intergration: Setting the context. In J.C. Norcross & M.R. Goldried (Eds.), *Handbook of psychotherapy integration* (pp. 3-45). New York: Basic Books.

Norcross, J.C., & Prochaska, J.O. (1988). A study of eclectic and integrative views revisited. *Professional Psychology, 19,* 170-174.

Norcross, J.C., & Thomas, B.L. (1988). What's stopping us now? Obstacles to psychotherapy integration. *Journal of Integrative and Eclectic Psychotherapy, 7,* 74-80.

Pallak, M., Cummings, N., Dorken, H., & Hanke, C. (1995). Effect of mental health treatment on medical costs. *Mind Body Medicine, 1,* 7-12.

Pipal, J.E. (1995). Managed Care, An Expose. *Psychotherapy,* 323-332.

Prochaska, J.O., DiClemente, C.C., & Norcross, J.C. (1992). In search of how people change. *American Psychologist, 47,* 1102-1114.

Prochaska, J.O., Norcross, J.C., & DiClemente, C.C. (1994). *Changing for Good.* William Morrow & Company: New York.

Rainer, J.P. (1996). Introduction to the special issue on psychotherapy outcomes. *Psychotherapy, 33,* 159.

Robinson, P. (1998). Behavioral Health Services in Primary Care: A New Perspective for Treating Depression. *Clinical Psychology Science and Practice, 5,* 77-93.

Seligman, M.E.P. (1995), The effectiveness of psychotherapy: *The Consumer Reports* study. *American Psychologist, 50,* 965-974.

Simon, G., Ormel, J., Vankorff, M., & Barlow, W. (1995).Health care costs associated with depressive and anxiety disorders in primary care. *American Journal of Psychiatry, 152,* 352-357.

Strupp, H.H. (1996). The tripartite model and the *Consumer Reports* study. *American Psychologist, 51,* 1017-1024.

Taylor, S.E., & Brown, J.D. (1988). Illusion and well-being: A social psychological perspective on mental health. *Psychological Bulletin, 103,* 193-210.

Watson, A.L., & Sher, K.J. Resolution of Alcohol Problems Without Treatment: Methodological Issues and Future Directions of Natural Recovery Research. *Clinical Psychology Science and Practice*, 5, 13-18.
Zimet, C. (1989) The mental health care revolution: Will psychology survive? *American Psychologist, 44*, 703-708.

Managed Care and Institutional Change: Considerations for the Private Practitioner

Tony D. Crespi, EdD
Anthony J. Giuliano, PhD

SUMMARY. Managed care has profoundly changed the health care system. Institutional downsizing, mergers, and acquisitions have occurred throughout the health care system and managed care organizations have deeply penetrated the health care market. With remarkable rapidity, these changes have put substantial pressures on private practitioners and are reshaping the focus and organization of private practice. Unfortunately, many practitioners lack a differentiated understanding of the practice implications of these changes, as well as practical strategies around which they might reorganize their professional practice. This paper examines the relationship between managed care and professional practice, providing the practitioner with a brief overview of key themes and ten foci around which service delivery can be reorganized. *[Article copies available for a fee from The Haworth Document Delivery Service: 1-800-342-9678. E-mail address: getinfo@haworthpressinc.com <Website: http://www.haworthpressinc.com>]*

KEYWORDS. Managed care, private practice, independent practice

---

Tony D. Crespi is Associate Professor of Psychology, The University of Hartford. He is a Licensed Psychologist, Licensed Marriage and Family Therapist, Certified School Psychologist, and Certified School Counselor.

Anthony J. Giuliano is Assistant Professor of Psychology, The University of Hartford. He is a Licensed Psychologist with specialty interests in Clinical Neuropsychology.

Address correspondence to: Dr. Tony D. Crespi, Department of Psychology, The University of Hartford, 200 Bloomfield Avenue, West Hartford, CT 06117.

[Haworth co-indexing entry note]: "Managed Care and Institutional Change: Considerations for the Private Practitioner." Crespi, Tony D., and Anthony J. Giuliano. Co-published simultaneously in *Critical Strategies: Psychotherapy in Managed Care* (The Haworth Press, Inc.) Vol. 1, No. 1, 2000, pp. 71-85; and: *Psycho-Economics: Managed Care in Mental Health in the New Millennium* (ed: Robert D. Weitz) The Haworth Press, Inc., 2000, pp. 71-85. Single or multiple copies of this article are available for a fee from The Haworth Document Delivery Service [1-800-342-9678, 9:00 a.m. - 5:00 p.m. (EST). E-mail address: getinfo@haworthpressinc.com].

The industrialization of mental health services, particularly in the form of managed care organizations, has profoundly altered contemporary mental health practice. At present the entire concept of fee-for-service practice is no longer the dominant mode for health care service and reimbursement. Managed care, a for-profit system, has emerged as dominant over the preexisting not-for-profit service provision system (Claxton, Feder, Shactman, & Altman, 1997).

Taken globally, the entire health care system is rapidly becoming organized around the business principles of managed care such as cost, efficiency, and accountability (Bobbitt, Marques, & Trout, 1998). These rapidly emerging currents clearly portend a future that is discontinuous with past practice strategies.

Benedict and Phelps (1998) note that managed care is, generally, a collective term which refers to the cost-containment strategies and financial arrangements which dominate health care service delivery in the United States. While managed care is not new, having begun with the Kaiser Permanente Medical Care Program in California in 1933 (a plan that singularly enrolls more than 6 million members; Belar, 1995), the changes wrought by the enlarged scope of this profit-making system are profoundly reshaping the private practices of mental health professionals.

Looking at this transformed arena, the reach of impact of managed care might best be appreciated when observing the extent to which Americans rely on their employers to provide health benefits. It has been reported, for instance, that managed care now covers 75% of those Americans who receive their health benefits from their jobs and the number continues to climb steadily (Prochaska & Norcross, 1999). Moreover, Norcross and his colleagues report that the median percentages of managed care patients in psychologists' caseloads alone escalated from 5% to 50% in only five years (1993-1998; see Norcross, Karg, & Prochaska, 1997).

With these changes, ranging from the demise of a fee-for-service model, to this managed care, for-profit, model, has emerged rising levels of distress among mental health professionals (Hersch, 1995), particularly those professionals steeped in traditional practice paradigms. Many mental health professionals committed to providing psychotherapy services feel unprepared and uncertain about the future (Austad, Sherman, & Holstein, 1993). Such emotions are not surprising given the methods by which managed care has begun to impact the provision of psychotherapy (e.g., restricting access to treatment, limiting the amount of psychotherapy, frequent utilization review, approval favoring short-term, symptom-focused psychotherapies, referrals through primary care physicians, restricting patient choice in providers and/or treatments; Prochaska & Norcross, 1999). In addition, this new environment is far more competitive (Crane, 1995), has exerted a negative impact on practice (Phelps, Eisman, & Kohout, 1998), and, with an emphasis on business interests has produced complex pressures to compromise the ethical provision of quality care (e.g., utilization review, financial incentives, threats to confidentiality; Rothbaum, Bernstein, Haller, Phelps, & Kohout, 1998).

Overall private practice remains in a state of considerable transition and some practices are, no doubt, in frank jeopardy. In fact, it has been predicted that solo private practices will become increasingly rare (Cummings & Dorken, 1986; Dorken & Cummings, 1991).

How can mental health professionals cope with such rapid and pervasive changes? What strategies are available to maintain viability in this labile system? How will lower cost providers such as master's-level clinicians compete against doctoral clinicians? What can practitioners do to diversify or revitalize their private practices? The questions facing mental health professionals are important and challenging. This paper, fundamentally, is intended to examine these critical issues, as well as provide mental health professionals clear, specific, strategies for reorganization.

HEALTH CARE REFORM

Changes in disease patterns, an aging population, an increase in costs associated with violence, and a growing lower class reflect a sampling of variables associated with the increasing costs of health care (Crane, 1995). Of course, health care costs have rapidly accelerated throughout the United States during the past decade (Weissenstein, 1993), and have only recently begun to slow.

Crane (1995) noted that health care services must limit costs to survive. However, despite the fact that mental health services actually account for only 10% of health care spending (Welch, 1993), the changes impacting both institutions and private practices are profound. Drainoni, Strickler, and Omans (1995) reported, for example, that 27 hospitals providing services for individuals with mental illness were scheduled to be closed within a single year. At the same time, mergers, acquisitions, and downsizing have also occurred *within* the managed care system itself, with more than 20 plans in the health maintenance organization experiencing organizational realignments in 1993 alone (Belar, 1995).

However, the scope of these changes is not limited solely to psychiatric hospitals and private practices. Indeed, the changes impacting health care are pervasive. For example, school-based health care is witnessing explosive growth in the form of school-based health clinics. Already, from approximately 100 school-based health clinics a decade ago there has been an increase to more than 900 school-based clinics today (Murray, 1997).

At the same time that such widespread changes have been unfolding, the actual need for mental health services has *not* decreased. Looking at children and adolescents, for example, there is an extreme need for mental health services. Of the 19 million adolescents between the ages 10 and 14, for instance, approximately 20% live below the poverty line, as many as 1 in 7 adolescents have no health insurance, and perhaps one quarter of adolescents are at risk for behaviors which can impact health (Carnegie Council on Adolescent Development, 1996). More specifically, children are experiencing widespread problems ranging from disintegrating families to drug abuse, depression, and physical abuse (Crane, 1995).

In terms of overall well-being, Jones (1995) notes that well-adjusted youth are becoming a minority and Ysseldyke, Dawson, Lehr, Reschly, Reynolds, and Telzrow (1997) have documented that students entering school at this time are more in need of mental health services than at any other time in our nation's recent history. Still, there is actually a *shortage* of mental health professionals specifically trained to address the needs of children (Culbertson, 1993). And, in fact, this is not new. Tuma (1989) noted approximately a decade ago that fewer than 1% of psychologists were practicing with children.

Similar arguments have been advanced to promote awareness of the discrepancy between need and service provision among many elderly people. As a result of the changing demography of our nation's population, the needs of the elderly often go unmet or are only poorly met, due in part to inadequate numbers of specialty trained clinicians. What this means, then, is that in a fundamental fashion, children, adolescents, the elderly, and families possess significant unmet needs for comprehensive mental health services.

At the same time that this need for services for children and families has actually increased, managed care has substantially changed the health care delivery system. Preauthorization requirements, provider network composition, payment amounts and terms, and benefit plans represent a sampling of areas which managed care has changed from the traditional fee for-service programs. Further, while treatment of the mentally ill often requires long-term treatment, Health Maintenance Organizations (HMOs) typically stipulate outpatient visits, which often, advertently or inadvertently, restricts services to patients with chronic illnesses. In fact, the American Psychiatric Association (1997) notes that the move to managed care for public sector programs poses significant risks for children and families. How, then, can mental health professionals remain viable during this time of such volatility?

MAINTAINING VIABILITY IN PROFESSIONAL PRACTICE

Within this cost-focused era, numerous changes have and are occurring. One change has been an increased interest, by managed groups, in the value of master's-level providers. Crane (1995) notes that master's degree providers can be paid lower salaries than doctoral providers, which can be very appealing to payers. Still, what does this mean to the Licensed Psychologist armed with a Ph.D. or Psy.D.? In general, it appears likely that doctoral mental health providers will increasingly be serving in administrative and consultative roles as psychotherapists while those with a master's degree become the predominate providers of psychotherapy (Cummings, 1995; Humphreys, 1996). Whatever one's preferences may have been, the debate about whether subdoctoral professionals should be conducting psychotherapy is over; as nearly all commentators have observed in recent years, psychotherapy will increasingly be performed by master's level clinicians.

For those who remain in private practice in some form, clinicians can expect greater emphasis by managed care groups on increasing profits while maintaining–or, rather, containing and reducing–costs. In general, this means practitioners will find a greater emphasis on practice diversification (Hersch, 1995), increasing need to join provider networks (Murphy, DeBernardo, & Shoemaker, 1998), decreased inpatient coverages (Giles & Marafiote, 1998), increased emphasis on practice guidelines and outcome measures (Bobbitt, Marques, & Trout, 1998), a challenging emphasis on empirically supported treatment protocols (Shueman, 1997), as well as a general privatization of once public sector health practices (Phelps, Eisman, & Kohout, 1998). Prochaska and Norcross (1999) summarized these emerging directions this way: ". . . in the new millennium, psychotherapy will increasingly be performed in the public marketplace by subdoctoral professionals for briefer intervals and according to practice guidelines. Some clinicians will find opportunities in the transformation, while others will abhor the change, but all will be profoundly influenced by these socio-economic forces" (p. 520).

Overall, such information suggests that practitioners who remain in private practice will face a much more challenging and competitive climate than what was evident as recently as 1990. Already, the evidence of key changes is glaring. In San Diego, for example, three major health maintenance organizations (HMOs) already provide care for over 90% of the population with health insurance (Patterson & Scherger, 1995), providing key evidence of the market penetration of managed care, and the mergers occurring within the managed care system.

What specifically can therapists in private practice explore to maintain viability amidst this volatility? The following section highlights several considerations for broadening professional options–and opportunities; however, it must be understood that each involves some reconceptualization of the traditional professional identity derived from typical training curricula of the past half-century.

1. Create Partnerships With Master's Degreed Providers

Given that practitioners with master's degrees are fiscally less expensive than doctoral level providers (Crane, 1995), practitioners might consider forming partnerships between doctoral *and* master's degreed providers to create diverse, complementary, and cost-effective mental health services.

A Licensed Psychologist, for instance, in partnership with a Licensed Marriage and Family Therapist, might find increased opportunities for niche marketing and practice opportunities. Alternatively, a Licensed Psychologist with specialty education and training and well-developed skills in one or more empirically supported treatments for particular disorders or client problems would likely provide a significant opportunity for master's level clinicians who do not graduate with similar training.

2. Develop Sufficient Understanding of Empirically Supported Treatments and Practice Guidelines

Though reportedly not developed as prescriptive standards of care, many commentators have observed that managed care organizations are likely to rely increasingly on practice guidelines in determining which treatments to approve and reimburse (Nathan, 1998; Prochaska & Norcross, 1999).

While their strengths and limitations are likely to remain a matter of considerable debate, it will likely behoove practitioners to develop a working understanding of their contents, methods, and sources of evidence (see Division 12 Task Force, 1995, which identified 22 "well-established," treatments for 21 different DSM-IV disorders).

The emphasis on established treatment outcomes seems particularly challenging in light of recent survey data that has revealed that the majority of clinical psychology training programs do not provide specific instruction in currently empirically-supported treatments (Crits-Christoph, Chambless, Frank, Brody, & Karp, 1995). At this point in time, these guidelines appear to highlight cognitive-behavioral interventions which may, inadvertently, constrain other practices, not so much because of negative findings but because of the relative absence of randomized, controlled clinical trials involving other therapy approaches (Nathan, 1998).

For those interested in developing expertise in this area, two especially useful resources in this regard can be found in Nathan and Gorman (1997) and Van Hasselt and Hersen (1996). Reading alone, however, is not sufficient for ethical and competent practice; rather, specific instruction and supervised training are required to insure these goals.

3. Develop and Maintain a Working Understanding of Psychopharmacology

Given that pharmacologic treatment is often combined with psychotherapy for many patients, it is critical that nonprescribing professionals achieve and maintain a working knowledge of the therapeutic and adverse effects of psychopharmacologic treatments (as well as other drug therapies for medical patients).

Piazza (1997) has argued, not only will quality of care be improved by active management of clients on psychotropic medication, but working relationships between nonprescribing practitioners and physicians or nurse practitioners will be enhanced. Piazza recommends, for example, that clinicians review all medications on intake, monitor the patient's responses (therapeutic and side effects) and adherence during treatment, and consult with medical doctors as needed.

In essence, Piazza makes a case for such activities in terms of legal rights and clinical responsibilities, and thus calls for training in psychopharmacology and the ready availability of appropriate drug reference materials.

4. Develop Diversified Arenas for Professional Practice

Mental health service provision is not the only option available to most well-trained licensed psychologists. Increasingly, private practitioners are working in multiple professional arenas. That is, an increasing number of practitioners blend a private practice in psychotherapy with part-time teaching, training, and consultation.

To remain viable in the 21st century, a practitioner who actively explores practice opportunities in different arenas can often find enhanced job security. Potential opportunities working with police or fire departments, for instance, providing recruit screening, employee assistance, and adjustment-focused psychotherapy, is illustrative of one option. Case consultation and/or focused skill-based training workshops to human service agencies or groups who lack psychologist colleagues represent another opportunity. In essence, the practitioner able to cultivate multiple contracts, involving practice in different settings, using different strands of professional expertise, can remain most viable, and minimize marginalization.

5. Develop Expertise in Behavioral Health Psychology

Pain management, stress reduction, wellness, weight control, and smoking cessation programs represent samples of the types of areas where practitioners with expertise in clinical health psychology can develop new practice opportunities.

Psychologists with expertise in behavioral health or medical psychology can provide a range of services for individuals with chronic health needs and for whom medical treatments are rarely sufficient by themselves, as well as for clients interested in health promotion or disease prevention programs. In addition to supervising or providing direct care to individual clients or small groups, doctoral-level psychologists are likely to function as experts in population-based interventions (Prochaska & Norcross, 1999).

For practitioners interested in enhancing this practice strand, such a shift will require a behavioral health focus, as well as a proactive practice model which can match therapeutic interventions to specific characteristics of the client and their stage of change. With such an approach, though, the practitioner is in a stronger position from which to lobby for increased interest from managed care organizations as this expertise continues to rise in validity and reliability.

6. Maximize Research and Statistical Expertise

As doctoral providers become involved in administration and program design (Belar, 1995), new opportunities arise to utilize doctoral-level research expertise in such areas as program evaluation and outcome research.

Practitioners interested in new practice opportunities can explore marketing program evaluation proposals detailing research and assessment methods and models to a range of potential clients including hospitals, nursing homes, health care businesses and organizations. Developing a capacity to conduct quasi-experimental studies with existing administrative data sets can be a very marketable skill. With large scale closures, mergers, and acquisitions in business, for example, the opportunity exists to offer expertise in such aspects as organizational analysis and program evaluation.

With a range of corporations and businesses requiring statistical and program evaluative expertise, the mental health professional competent in research, statistics, and program evaluation is well-armed to work in this important area of practice. While such work does not, typically, involve direct care, such services are viable, and fiscally lucrative.

7. Maximize Specialty Certifications and Credentials

Current reimbursement structures are clearly linked to professional credentials. State regulatory credentials as a Licensed Psychologist,

Licensed Marriage and Family Therapist, Licensed Clinical Social Worker, and Licensed Professional Counselor are examples of State Department of Health Services licenses critical to third-party reimbursement.

In addition to such established credentials, the practitioner should examine specialty certifications as such credentials are often desirable in providing insurance carriers and employers with evidence of specialty skills. The Licensed Psychologist, for example, who acquires the A.B.P.P. designation from the American Board of Professional Psychologists is one illustration of one advanced credential which has gained steady recognition from associations, insurance groups, as well as professional colleagues.

While the proliferation of specialty certifications itself raises new concerns as to how the public can remain knowledgeable about the growing battery of credentials being advertised and marketed as evidence of specialty skills, it is also true that specialty certifications can provide specific evidences of competencies. Private practitioners should highlight specialty credentials on stationary and in professional proposals for contractual employment.

8. Create Corporate Education and Training Opportunities

Corporate education and training is a large and growing expense for expansive professional opportunity. Too often mental health professionals, however, do not recognize the opportunity to contribute expertise through workshops, training institutes, and corporate education programs. Such areas as stress reduction, time management, conflict resolution strategies, race relations, gender sensitive supervision, and attending skills workshops represent samples of topics for inservice training many doctoral level health professionals are well equipped to conduct. To explore such opportunities, however, practitioners need to develop and market proposals to corporate clients and make use of existing professional and/or social networks.

Workplace violence, organizational closures, mergers, and downsizing have impacted a large segment of society. Virtually every Fortune 1000 company, for example, has already reported downsizing (Willis, 1987). In fact, between 1987 and 1991 it has been reported that more than 5 million peoples' jobs were impacted work force reductions (Hitt, Keats, Harback, & Nixon, 1994). For human resources personnel, such changes have produced enormous responsibilities for outplacement counseling and career workshops.

For mental health professionals, the opportunity to offer clinical expertise is inviting. Workshops and counseling opportunities exist in several areas including: career counseling, resume development, career transitions, strategic leadership, competitiveness and cooperation in the workplace, and staff redeployment. In addition, professionals with auxiliary credentials in business, such as those with an M.B.A., and those with certifications in such areas as career counseling, may be exceptionally well-poised to explore this arena.

While astute practitioners might benefit from strategic education and training utilizing business school opportunities, it would be myopic not to recognize that many practitioners are already well-versed with the professional skills to effectively solicit a range of differing business consulting opportunities. The first step, though, is to examine business needs, followed by the marketing of carefully designed corporate education and training workshops and inservice institutes.

9. Create Collaborative Relationships with Primary Care and Family Practice Professionals

Increasingly, new opportunities are emerging in primary care settings (Haley, McDaniel, Bray, Frank, Heldring, Johnson, Lu, Reed, & Wiggins, 1998). Medical schools, for example, are themselves an area with significant opportunity (Metarazzo, 1994).

Given reported weaknesses in behavioral management strategies in the medical system (Alto, 1995), mental health practitioners are well situated to emerge as leaders in this realm. However, to create these opportunities means creating collaborative relationships with primary care professionals (e.g., physicians, nurse practitioners, physicians' assistants). In addition to such arrangements, opportunities exist to teach and train residents, and work in a wide spectrum of areas, including: sleep disorders, rehabilitation, pediatrics, parent education, and eating disorders.

Psychologists interested in developing partnerships or co-practices with primary care and family medicine professionals, of course, are best able to effect such relationships if based on specialty training internships and post-doctoral residencies in academic medical centers, and when equipped with specific skills that complement the needs of primary care providers.

10. Examine Critical Areas of Need

Within mental health care there exist a number of critical areas of need which remain of great concern to society, as well as to business and industry. The cost of substance abuse, for instance, has increased markedly across companies.

Using alcoholism as an illustration of one area of need, it can be noted that with the exception of very severe alcoholism, Allen and Mattson (1993) note no advantage to inpatient over outpatient treatment for alcoholism. What this finding suggests is that private practitioners with expertise in treating alcoholism on an outpatient basis may be of appeal to managed care groups, as well as to companies with substance abuse programs. In the current market, these practitioners might benefit from actively marketing this practice skill and expertise.

While it can be challenging to monitor emerging and critical areas of need, such arenas as domestic violence, forensic psychology, health and wellness, AIDS education, addictions, psychology and public health, child care, as well as such areas as program evaluation represent a sampling of arenas in which mental health professionals can remain viable and productive as we enter the 21st century.

CONCLUSIONS

Dramatic changes in the health care system have provided an impetus and unique opportunity for adaptation in the identity and roles of psychologists. Primary care settings–medical schools for instance–are one area of opportunity (Haley, McDaniel, Bray, Frank, Heldring, Johnson, Lu, Reed, & Wiggins, 1998; Metarazzo, 1994).

In truth, the reality of a rapidly changing, managed-care driven health care marketplace indicates that the mental health professional must examine new opportunities to remain viable. In essence, to survive in private practice within an impermanent managed care marketplace practitioners need to increasingly understand the implications of the managed care system, and create new opportunities, partnerships and linkages which can maximize specific skills and abilities which characterize well-trained mental health professionals.

Clearly, managed care has transformed health care. Karon (1995) notes, for example, that managed care is almost universal in the United States. Fortunately, for the astute practitioner, there are a wide range of options to remain viable. In corporate America, for example, organizational closures, mergers, and downsizing have impacted a large segment of society. Virtually every Fortune 1000 company has already reported downsizing (Willis, 1987). Moreover, with more than 5 million people impacted by work force reductions (Hitt, Keats, Harback, & Nixon, 1994), corporate opportunities for intervention are extremely diverse and engaging.

Although not all practitioners will have the interest–nor possibly the need–to completely revamp professional practices, many practitioners must examine new and emerging markets to remain competitive. This integrative discussion on managed care, and on emerging practice opportunities, was initiated to provide a beginning template for change.

Professional psychologists, and mental health professionals in general, have extraordinary skills and abilities from which to impact society. Still, the independent practitioner must astutely examine new markets, new opportunities, and new marketing strategies. In this way, we can remain viable. To ignore the profound changes is to remain uncertain amidst continuing volatility. We think the latter is suffocating. The former invigorating. Put another way, mental health professionals need to adapt to survive. This discussion has suggested ten specific strategies for change. Based on the literature, based on managed care, based on an impermanent society, the profession must adapt to survive. It is a lesson of life.

REFERENCES

Allen, J., & Mattson, M. (1993). Strategies for the treatment of alcoholism. In T. Giles (Ed.), *Handbook of effective psychotherapy* (pp. 379-408). New York: Plenum.

Alto, W.A. (1995). Prevention in practice. *Primary Care, 22,* 543-554.

American Psychiatric Association. (1997). *Public mental health: A changing system in an era of managed care.* Washington, DC: Author.

Austad, C.S., Sherman, W.O., & Holstein, L. (1993). Psychotherapists in the HMO. *HMO Practice, 7,* 122-126.

Belar, C.D. (1995). Collaboration in capitated care: Challenges for psychology. *Professional Psychology: Research and Practice, 26,* 139-146.

Benedict, J.G., & Phelps, R. (1998). Introduction: Psychology's view of managed care. *Professional Psychology: Research and Practice, 29,* 29-30.

Bobbitt, B.L., Marques, C.C., & Trout, D.L. (1998). Managed behavioral health care: Current status, recent trends, and the role of psychology. *Clinical Psychology: Science and Practice, 5,* 53-65.

Carnegie Council on Adolescent Development. (1996, March). *Great transitions: Preparing adolescents for a new century.* New York: NY.

Claxton, G., Feder, J., Shactman, D., & Altman, S. (1997). Public policy issues in nonprofit conversions: An overview. *Health Affairs, 16*, 9-28.

Crane, D.R. (1995). Health care reform in the United States: Implications for training and practice in marriage and family therapy. *Journal of Marital and Family Therapy, 21*, 115-125.

Crits-Cristoph, P., Chambless, D.L., Frank, E., Brody, C., & Karp, J.F. (1995). Training in empirically validated treatments: What clinical psychology students are learning. *Professional Psychology: Research and Practice, 26*, 514-522.

Culbertson, J.L. (1993). Clinical child psychology in the 1990's: Broadening our scope. *Journal of Clinical Child Psychology, 22*, 116-122.

Cummings, N.A. (1995). Impact of managed care on employment and training: A primer for survival. *Professional Psychology: Research and Practice, 26*, 10-15.

Cummings, N.A., & Dorken, H. (1986). Corporations, networks, and service plans: Economically sound models for practice. In H. Dorken & Associates (Eds.). *Professional psychology in transition* (pp. 165-174). San Francisco: Jossey-Bass.

Dorken, H., & Cummings, N.A. (1991). The potential effect on private practice of training in targeted focussed mental health treatment for a specific population: A brief report. *Psychotherapy in Private Practice, 9*, 45-51.

Division 12 Task Force. (1995). Training in and dissemination of empirically-validated psychological treatments: Report and recommendations. *The Clinical Psychologist, 48*, 3-23.

Drainoni, M., Strickler, G., & Omans, J. (1995). Redeployment of staff from state institutions: Issues for state health policy-makers. *Administration and Policy in Mental Health, 22*, 553-562.

Giles, T.R., & Marafiote, R.A. (1998). Managed care and the practitioner: A call for unity. *Clinical Psychology: Science and Practice, 5*, 41-50.

Haley, W.E., McDaniel, S.H., Bray, J.H., Frank, R.G., Heldring, M., Johnson, S.B., Lu, E.G., Reed, G.M., & Wiggins, J.G. (1998). Psychological practice in primary care settings: Practical tips for clinicians. *Professional Psychology: Research and Practice, 29*, 237-244.

Hersch, L. (1995). Adapting to health care reform and managed care: Three strategies for survival and growth. *Professional Psychology: Research and Practice, 26*, 16-26.

Hitt, M.A., Keats, B.W., Harback, H.F., & Nixon, R.D. (1994). Rightsizing: Building and maintaining strategic leadership and long-term competitiveness. *Organizational Dynamics, 23*, 18-32.

Humphreys, K. (1996). Clinical psychologists as psychotherapists: History, future, & alternatives. *American Psychologist, 51*, 190-197.

Jones, D.G. (1995, Summer). Youth gangs, public school systems, and the school psychologist. *The School Psychologist, 49*, 1,72,73,75.

Karon, B.P. (1995). Provision of psychotherapy under managed health care: A growing crisis and national nightmare. *Professional Psychology: Research and Practice, 26*, 5-9.

Metarazzo, J. (1994). Health and behavior: The coming together of science and practice in psychology and medicine after a century of benign neglect. *Journal of Clinical Psychology in Medical Settings, 1*, 7-39.

Murphy, M.J., DeBernardo, C.R., & Shoemaker, W.E. (1998). Impact of managed care on independent practice and professional ethics: A survey of independent practitioners. *Professional Psychology: Research and Practice, 29*, 43-51.

Murray, B. (1997, June). School-based health care is gaining in popularity. *APA Monitor 28*, p. 7.

Nathan, P. E. (1998). Practice guidelines: Not yet ideal. *American Psychologist, 53*, 290-299.

Nathan, P.E., & Gorman, J.M. (1997). *A guide to treatments that work*. New York: Oxford University Press.

Norcross, J.C., Karg, R.S., & Prochaska, J.O. (1997). Clinical psychologists and managed care: Some data from Division 12 membership. *The Clinical Psychologist, 50*, 4-8.

Patterson, J., & Scherger, J.E. (1995). A critique of health care reform in the United States: Implications for the training and practice of marriage and family therapy. *Journal of Marital and Family Therapy, 21*, 127-135.

Phelps, R., Eisman, E.J., & Kohout, J. (1998). Psychological practice and managed care: Results of the CAPP practitioner survey. *Professional Psychology: Research and Practice, 29*, 31-36.

Piazza, N.J. (1997). Managing clients on psychotropic medication: Guidelines for nonprescribing practitioners. *Essential Psychopharmacology 3*, 291-300.

Prochaska, J.O., & Norcross, J.C. (1999). *Systems of psychotherapy: A transtheoretical analysis (4th ed.)*. Pacific Grove, CA: Brooks/Cole.

Rothbaum, P.A., Bernstein, D.M., Haller, O., Phelps, R., & Kohout, J. (1998). New Jersey psychologists' report on managed mental health care. *Professional Psychology: Research and Practice, 29*, 37-42.

Shueman, S.A. (1997). Confronting health care realities: A reply to Sank (1997). *Professional Psychology: Research and Practice, 28*, 555-558.

Tuma, J.M. (1989). Mental health services for children: The state of the art. *American Psychologist, 44*, 188-199.

Van Hasselt, V. B., & Hesen, M. (Eds.) (1996). *Sourcebook of psychological treatment manuals for adult disorders*. New York: Plenum Press.

Weissenstein, L. (1993, January 11). Health spending hits $838 billion in 1992. *Modern Healthcare*, p. 2.

Welch, B.L. (1993, February). Spend mental health dollars more wisely, Welch says. *APA Monitor*, pp. 18-19.

Willis, R. (1987). What's happening to America's middle managers? *Management Review, 76*, 24-33.

Ysseldyke, J., Dawson, P., Lehr, C., Reschly, D., Reynolds, M., & Telzrow, C. (1997). *School psychology: A blueprint for training and practice II*. Bethesda, MD: National Association of School Psychologists.

Providing Mental Health Services at What Price? Ethical Issues and Dilemmas for Social Workers Practicing in a Managed Care Environment

Dawn Hall Apgar, MSW, LSW, ACSW

SUMMARY. The advent of managed care has raised many ethical issues for social workers. These issues relate to social workers' ethical responsibilities to their clients in the areas of self-determination, informed consent, competence, conflicts of interest, privacy and confidentiality, and the interruption and termination of services. Using the newly revised Code of Ethics of the National Association of Social Workers as a basis for discussion, this article identifies the issues and dilemmas facing social workers delivering services in a managed care environment. Formal and informal safeguards are provided for practitioners which will help them avoid ethical violations while protecting the integrity of their mental health treatment. *[Article copies available for a fee from The Haworth Document Delivery Service: 1-800-342-9678. E-mail address: getinfo@haworthpressinc.com <Website: http://www.haworthpressinc.com>]*

KEYWORDS. Private practice, ethics, social work practice, managed care, psychotherapy, practice

---

Dawn Hall Apgar is a Licensed Social Worker and a member of the Academy of Certified Social Workers. She is Assistant Director, Developmental Disabilities Planning Institute, New Jersey Institute of Technology, Newark, NJ. She is a doctoral candidate in social work at Rutgers University in New Brunswick, New Jersey.

Address correspondence to: Dawn Hall Apgar, 448 Old Main Street, Asbury, NJ 08802.

[Haworth co-indexing entry note]: "Providing Mental Health Services at What Price? Ethical Issues and Dilemmas for Social Workers Practicing in a Managed Care Environment." Apgar, Dawn Hall. Co-published simultaneously in *Critical Strategies: Psychotherapy in Managed Care* (The Haworth Press, Inc.) Vol. 1, No. 1, 2000, pp. 87-104; and: *Psycho-Economics: Managed Care in Mental Health in the New Millennium* (ed: Robert D. Weitz) The Haworth Press, Inc., 2000, pp. 87-104. Single or multiple copies of this article are available for a fee from The Haworth Document Delivery Service [1-800-342-9678, 9:00 a.m. - 5:00 p.m. (EST). E-mail address: getinfo@haworthpressinc.com].

Within the last two decades, managed health and mental health care in the United States has expanded exponentially. Given the escalating cost of fee-for-service medical and behavioral health care, almost every major corporation in the United states has implemented, or is considering moving towards, a managed health benefits program. It is not surprising, therefore, that the number of individuals enrolled in Health Maintenance Organizations (HMOs) has increased by over 500% since 1980 (Dow, 1993). Though it is argued that the advent of managed care yields no real savings and that this new system merely redistributes funds previously spent on client care to administrative expenses and profits, the appeal of managed care to act as a means by which to improve the efficiency of the present health and mental health systems is a strong one. Thus, it is likely that managed care will continue to prosper as an alternative to fee-for-service care, thereby causing some to estimate that 95% of mental health services will be provided through managed care systems by the turn of the century (NASW, 1994, p. 1).

This growth in managed mental health care is likely to further challenge social workers who are already struggling with the demands and restrictions placed upon them by managed care companies in light of the principles and standards of their own profession. The cost containment strategies employed by managed care companies are causing social workers to be become increasingly concerned about the issues of cost impinging on their clinical judgements. Social workers are caught between their own professionalism on one hand and the requirements of their livelihood on the other.

This article will review the major ethical issues and dilemmas facing social workers in their efforts to provide quality mental health treatment within a managed care environment. Whenever available, accounts of social workers currently providing services for managed care organizations will be included to highlight the presented material. The newly revised Code of Ethics of the National Association of Social Workers provides a framework for identification and discussion (NASW, 1996). Lastly, easily implemented strategies aimed at safeguarding against ethical violations will be supplied for practicing social workers.

THE CODE OF ETHICS OF THE NATIONAL ASSOCIATION OF SOCIAL WORKERS

A code of ethics is a distinguishing factor between a profession and a trade or business (Elpers & Abbott, 1992, p. 437). It represents a

profession's self-image and the moral wisdom of its experienced practitioners (Sabin, 1994, p. 318). "Perhaps more importantly, it gives at
least an implicit picture of the profession's view of what it means to be
a virtuous professional. As such it offers itself as a template for the
clinician's professional ego ideal and for education of the next generation of professionals" (Sabin, 1994, p. 318). As professional roles
change, ethical codes must be reevaluated and revised. Recently, at a
meeting of the Delegate Assembly of the National Association of
Social Workers, two hundred and ninety-three social workers, repre-
senting the association's 155,000 members, adopted a new Code of
Ethics which sets forth standards of ethical behavior to guide social
workers in their professional relationships. The NASW Code of Ethics, which had not been comprehensively revamped since its adoption
in 1979, "is intended to serve as a guide to the everyday professional
conduct of social workers" (NASW, 1996, p. i). Though not prescriptive in providing behavioral protocols for all situations, the Code of
Ethics "establishes a set of specific ethical standards that should be
used to guide social work practice" (NASW, 1996, p. 2). In addition, it
helps "social workers identify relevant considerations when professional obligations conflict or ethical uncertainties arise" (NASW,
1996, p. 2). As such, the Code of Ethics of NASW must be used by all
social workers against which to judge the appropriateness of practice
standards.

The requirements and demands placed upon social workers delivering mental health services for managed care companies vary slightly
as do the companies' cost containment strategies. It is, therefore, likely that the magnitude of the ethical dilemmas experienced by social
workers working with these managed care organizations will differ
somewhat depending upon the aforementioned factors. However, by
most accounts, the types of ethical issues facing social workers in all
managed care contexts are the same, specifically those relating to
social workers' ethical responsibilities to their clients in the areas of
self-determination, informed consent, competence, conflicts of interest, privacy and confidentiality, and the interruption and termination
of services (Blum, 1992; NASW, 1994; Schreter et al., 1994). Thus, it
is necessary to specifically examine some of the prevailing issues in
managed care which are likely to cause conflict for social workers in
light of the ethical standards established by their profession.

NASW ETHICAL STANDARDS
Social Workers' Ethical Responsibilities to Their Clients

1.02 Self-Determination
"Social workers respect and promote the right of clients to self-determination and assist clients in their efforts to identify and clarify their goals. Social workers may limit clients' right to self-determination when, in the social workers' professional judgement, clients' actions or potential actions pose a serious, foreseeable, and imminent risk to themselves or others" (NASW, 1996, p. 7).

In an effort to contain costs, managed care companies limit the types and lengths of covered treatments. Since many individuals cannot afford services which are not paid for by their managed care plans, this truly restricts the scope of treatment options available to them. Consequently, social workers, as providers for managed care companies, may be inclined to discuss with their clients only those treatments which are included as part of their plans. However, this is inappropriate if they represent only a portion of the options available. Practitioners must review all clinically appropriate treatment options with clients, the costs of such treatments, and whether or not they are covered by their HMOs or Preferred Provider Organizations (PPOs). In no way should practitioners' enrollment in HMOs or PPOs influence their judgement about necessary and appropriate alternatives for clients. When desired treatment is not covered, social workers must inform their clients of this problem and assist them by advocating with their managed care companies or by finding other appropriate treatment resources (Gottlieb, 1992).

1.03 Informed Consent
"Social workers should provide services to clients only in the context of a professional relationship based, when appropriate, on valid informed consent. Social workers should use clear and understandable language to inform clients of the purpose of the services, risks related to the services, limits to services because of the requirements of a third-party payer, relevant costs, reasonable alternatives, clients' right to refuse or withdraw consent, and the time frame covered by the consent. Social workers should provide clients with an opportunity to ask questions" (NASW, 1996, pp. 7-8).

From the onset, clients must be informed of the purposes of, and limitations to, the services that they will be receiving, including the confines of treatment which may be imposed by their managed care companies. The need to discuss the time limits and restrictions of treatment before such therapies have even begun can cause problems in practitioner-client relationships for several reasons. Clients can be angered by the restrictions imposed upon them, stemming from misinformation or false advertising by their managed care companies. In addition, clients can experience anger transferred from practitioners who are upset with the perceived limitations to their professional discretion placed upon them by HMOs and PPOs. Therefore, it is imperative that practitioners be aware of, and resolve, their own feelings about providing services within a managed care environment so that these feelings are not inappropriately imposed on their clients.

One care manager working at a major managed care company reports that clients routinely call her claiming that their chosen therapists spend at least half of initial sessions complaining about the managed care company. This flagrant misuse of therapeutic time has caused some managed care companies to impose "gag rules" which prevent providing therapists from making defamatory remarks about them to clients. Though this imposition of "gag rules" is the center of much debate, social work practitioners must remember that they are obligated to explain the scope and limitations of benefits to their clients objectively and professionally. Thus, they must restrain from imposing their own feelings into these conversations as they are inappropriate and can damage the effectiveness of therapeutic relationships.

Obtaining the informed consent of clients referred by managed care companies also poses ethical dilemmas for social work practitioners. All too often, clients are so distressed by the situations which have forced them into treatment that they are too overwhelmed to rationally consider the restrictions imposed on them by their managed care companies. A social worker in private practice recalls her own struggles with this issue:

> I routinely reviewed clients' benefits with them during their first sessions with me. This explanation included the numbers of sessions which had been authorized by their managed care companies. In every case, clients always chose to pursue treatment under these limitations. However, inevitably, about half way through the number of authorized sessions, benefit limitations

would again become an issue as I would remind clients of where we were in the course of treatment. Often, my clients would tell me that they had paid little attention to what I had told them pertaining to benefit levels during their initial visits with me as they were consumed by their own problems and were just happy to have someone with whom to talk. These comments started to bother me as a therapist as I questioned whether clients could really understand the scope of their benefits during periods when they were so distressed by what was going on in their lives.

When working with managed care companies, social workers will need to employ informed consent procedures that may not otherwise be required. For example, Gottlieb (1992) urges practitioners to inform clients in all cases of their benefits at the onset of assessment or treatment even if employers or managed care companies have already done so. He suggests that, whenever possible, this be done during initial telephone screenings. Oftentimes clients are unaware or misinformed of the benefits available to them so it is critical that social work practitioners provide current, clear, and accurate information to them (DeLeon et al., 1991). Also, as mentioned, practitioners must resolve their own anger or hostile feelings towards managed care companies as these feelings may unconsciously be transferred to clients and, subsequently, affect their decisions with regard to the course of treatment. Disclosed information must also include any financial arrangements with managed care companies which could affect treatment recommendations and/or planning, such as provisions for fee splitting, referral fees, or financial incentive for less intensive treatment (Gottlieb, 1992).

> ***1.04 Competence***
> "Social workers should provide services and represent themselves as competent only within the boundaries of their education, training, license, certification, consultation received, supervised experience, or other relevant professional experience" (NASW, 1996, p. 8).

Often managed care companies adopt particular theoretical orientations or treatment models upon which decisions with regard to the courses and lengths of treatments are based (Bak et al., 1991). The onus is, therefore, on social workers to dialogue with managed care companies and determine the theoretical orientations upon which treatment decisions are made. Social workers must avoid working with managed care companies who will not readily disclose their treatment models as it is impossible for them to practice competently and ethically without adequate knowledge of the boundaries under which they are expected to function (Gottlieb, p. 486).

Ethical violations occur when social workers agree to practice utilizing treatment models in which they have not been adequately trained. For example, social workers trained and experienced in long-term insight-oriented therapy must not agree to provide treatment for managed care companies who operate under brief therapy models. In addition, social work practitioners must not attempt to treat clients with problems which are outside the scope of their expertise. A social worker who is a provider for a large managed care company recalls,

> I received a call from a man who had many trans-gender issues and wanted to begin therapy to address them. I told him that I was not trained in this area and asked him how he had obtained my name. He told me that I was highly recommended by his managed care company and that he had chosen me based on their recommendation. I was perplexed since I had never indicated any training or past experience in this area. Before hanging up, I gave him the name of a therapist who I knew specialized in treating such issues and he assured me that he would call her. About an hour later, I received a call from someone at his managed care company, urging me to consider treating this man as he lived in my area and was anxious to find a provider near his home. I told her that I couldn't provide service to him as I had no special training or experience in treating trans-gender issues. She was a little indignant and treated me like the only problem with her request was my own resistance. I felt like she was thinking 'What kind of therapist are you? You can't even help this guy who needs you,' though she never actually said it.

As illustrated, often in managed care environments, social work practitioners feel pressured to serve all those who cross their paths. These pressures can come from external factors such as tangible incidents with managed care companies in which practitioners are pushed to take clients whose problems are outside of their training and expertise, or be self-imposed resulting from internal beliefs that cost containment is so important to managed care companies that the quality of clients' care will be compromised in order to limit costs. Whatever the source, practitioners may consider working with those whose problems are beyond their expertise and training. Ten common sub-standards or rationalizations that social workers use to justify practicing beyond their competence in a managed care environment include:

1. I may not have actually treated someone with that problem, but I know many therapists who have and they can help me if I need it.
2. I am not all that hot, but I am all they've got.
3. I am just trying to help someone in need.
4. I know a lot of therapists who do the same thing.
5. I know that I can help this client.
6. I told my client that I hadn't treated that problem before, but he/she only wanted therapy from me.
7. I really feel connected with my client. It would take another therapist a long time to develop such a relationship. This would mean time wasted on not treating the problem.
8. Others, including the managed care company, think that I am qualified so I must be.
9. No other therapist has any more specialized expertise than I do in this area.
10. I don't think that there are any specific training programs for this kind of problem so I guess that means that I already know enough to treat it. (Adapted from Pope & Vasquez, 1991)

It is essential that social workers monitor their own practices to ensure that none of the aforementioned rationalizations are used to justify inappropriate treatment. Therapists must have the proper training and experience to justify that they are the most appropriate clinicians to help clients. Self-assessment is especially critical for therapists who may feel the described undue pressures to practice beyond the scope of their expertise. Haas and Malouf (1989) suggest that therapists ask themselves the following questions when assessing their own competence:

1. What kind of specialized training have you received? Do you have a practice specialty or sub-specialty? Do relevant practice standards exist and are you following them? Do you have the

designated licenses or credentials within your practice specialty or sub-specialty?

2. Are you familiar with research and theoretical findings in your areas of practice? Do you search the literature and consult with colleagues to keep current on the research of your specialty?
3. Are you the most appropriate person to help the client? If not, what can you do to get consultation on the case or refer it to a more appropriate professional?
4. Are you emotionally able to help the client? Do you have a good referral network available for cases you do not feel comfortable treating? Do you limit your practice to only those cases that you feel competent to handle?
5. Could you justify your decisions to treat or other practice decisions to a group of your peers?

1.06 Conflicts of Interest

"Social workers should be alert to and avoid conflicts of interest that interfere with the exercise of professional discretion and impartial judgement. Social workers should inform clients when a real or potential conflict of interest arises and take reasonable steps to resolve the issue in a manner that makes the clients' interests primary and protects clients' interests to the greatest extent possible. In some cases, protecting clients' interests may require termination of the professional relationship with proper referral of the client" (NASW, 1996, p. 9).

Newman and Brickman (1991) contend that therapists providing mental health services through managed care companies are at high risk for conflicts of interest since they have loyalties both to clients to whom they are providing treatment and managed care companies who are paying their bills. The relationships between providers, managed care companies, and clients have raised questions about for whom providing professionals actually work–their patients or the managed care organizations (Geraty, Hendren, & Flaa, 1992, p. 399). Whatever the answer, social workers cannot deny that there are no longer alone with their clients in therapy consultation rooms, but instead share this turf with their clients' managed care companies. Though this is true of all services which are paid for by a third party, the primary interest of managed care companies to cut costs creates increased difficulties for social work practitioners attempting to maintain their practices. All too often social workers tell of incidents where they have not received any further referrals from managed care companies with whom they advocated for additional client services. Thus, the practitioner-client-managed care relationship is one which has inherent conflicts of interest for social workers who must often choose between upholding the ethical standards of their profession and maintaining a source of client referrals which is key to their livelihood.

Stromberg et al. (1988) caution that the vulnerability of practitioners to compromise their clients' welfare is likely to increase as social workers compete with each other in a shrinking marketplace. This is compounded by the fact that managed care creates specific incentives, namely those of doing less (Sederer & St.Clair, 1989). One provider group, concerned with instilling a "managed care sensibility" in their clinical staff, reports establishing minimum performance targets for practitioners and rewarding work performance in excess of these targets with cash bonuses (Psychotherapy Finances, 1996). This incentive system greatly rewards therapists for initial sessions and group therapy, thereby discouraging practitioners from treating clients any longer than necessary and discouraging individual sessions since they "can make as much money conducting one group session as they can seeing four or five patients individually" (Psychotherapy Finances, 1996, pp. 5-6). Interestingly, however, quality care and client satisfaction are not part of the provider's system and while minimum levels of satisfaction are expected, they are not rewarded as part of the plan.

Although under these circumstances, it is questionable whether professional discretion and impartial judgement can fully be exercised by social work practitioners, it is estimated that nearly all mental health services will be provided through managed care systems by the turn of the century. Thus, social workers must determine ways to deliver treatment ethically within the unpleasant realities of this environment. Supervision and increased education for social work students and practitioners in the area of ethics must be provided. Schools of social work and continuing education programs must prioritize intensive instruction on the ethical standards of the profession as well as specific training in ethical problem-solving. Only through these means will social workers develop the knowledge base and self-awareness necessary to operate ethically under such conditions.

1.07 Privacy and Confidentiality

"Social workers should not solicit private information from clients unless it is essential to providing services or conducting social work evaluation or research . . . Social workers may disclose confidential information when appropriate with valid consent from a client, or a person legally authorized to consent on behalf of a client . . . Social workers should inform clients, to the extent possible, about the disclosure of confidential information and the potential consequences, when feasible before the disclosure is made . . . Social workers should not disclose confidential information to third part payers unless clients have authorized such disclosure" (NASW, 1996, pp. 10-11).

Confidentiality is considered a major tenet of the social work profession. Central to all practitioner-client relationships is a trust that information revealed in the course of treatment will not be disclosed without proper authorization from clients. With limited exceptions to the policy of strict confidentiality (i.e., in instances to prevent serious, foreseeable, and imminent harm to clients or other identifiable persons), the protection of confidential information is determined by both practitioners and their clients. However, once mental health practitioners began to receive reimbursement from insurance companies, a third party was added to the professional relationship (Gottlieb, 1992, p. 482). In the case of managed care, this third party often wants extensive information about clients' problems as well as the courses of treatment in order to justify continued therapy costs. Though the release of this information may be necessary for continued payment of treatment, it can also jeopardize the welfare of clients in cases where unwarranted information is requested or managed care companies' policies for processing confidential information are not adequate.

For example, one managed care company required its providers to include information about clients' earnings and financial status on its evaluation forms. This same company also required practitioners to provide information about any past client convictions for driving under influence of drugs or alcohol. Though the company eventually dropped these items from its evaluation forms after being informed by providers that collecting and sharing this information violated ethical standards, such requests by managed care companies are not uncommon and can cause problems for social workers providing services within these settings (Blum, 1992).

Other problems associated with client confidentiality and privacy involve the transmission of information between practitioners and managed care companies. Often practitioners have to call managed care companies to obtain approvals for extended care or authorizations for client referrals. When placing these calls, social workers may be fooled into believing that they are speaking to other professionals who have been trained in the safeguarding of confidential information. However, this may be a misconception as frequently only technicians who function in an administrative or clerical capacity answer the telephones and process such requests. It is, therefore, essential that social workers only identify their reason for calling without releasing vital case information and ask to speak to appropriate care managers who are professionals with the authority to approve session extensions or referrals. Only when social workers are sure that they are talking to professional personnel should they release confidential information.

Often managed care companies request case notes for the purpose of utilization review. Fearing such requests, some social work practitioners have been reluctant to keep records which would violate client confidentiality if released. Though this is unethical and poor practice, it clearly illustrates the fear and conviction of social workers in the area of client confidentiality. Gottlieb (1992) suggests a better strategy for handling this difficult situation. He contends that raw data, such as case notes, belong to practitioners and should not be released. However, with clients' authorization, treatment summaries or forms that managed care companies use for this purpose can be prepared as acceptable alternatives (Gottlieb, 1992, p. 483). The completion of these summaries meets the needs of the managed care companies while still protecting the privacy rights of clients.

In order to minimize ethical dilemmas with regard to client confidentiality, social workers should adhere to the following guidelines in their work with managed care:

1. Obtain and review the managed care company's policy regarding confidentiality prior to becoming a provider. Does the managed care company tape telephone conversations with providers? If

so, for what purpose and who has access to these tapes? What written information is required by the managed care company? Who has access to this information? Practitioners must advocate for change if current policies are not acceptable.

2. Obtain the client's written consent before releasing any information to the managed care company. Ensure that the release clearly specifies what information is to be released, the means by which it is to be released (i.e., over the phone, sent through the mail, etc.), and the time period for which the release is authorized (i.e., can information only be released one time or on an on-going basis for 2 months, 4 months, etc.).

3. Inform the client each time information is released to the managed care company and have the client review released materials. Never fax client information to managed care companies as it is impossible to ensure that such information will not be seen by those not authorized to view it. Complete reports with clients or review your written responses with them as this often generates material which can be used later in treatment.

1.15 Interruption of Services/1.16 Termination of Services
"Social workers should make reasonable efforts to ensure continuity of services in the event that they are interrupted by factors such as unavailability, relocation, illness, disability, or death" (NASW, 1996, p. 14). "Social workers should take reasonable steps to avoid abandoning clients who are still in need of services. Social workers should withdraw services precipitously only under unusual circumstances, giving careful consideration to all factors in the situation and taking care to minimize possible adverse effects. Social workers should assist in making appropriate arrangements for continuation of services when necessary" (NASW, 1996, p. 15).

Important issues arise when there are breaks in treatment or treatment is unjustly terminated. Interruption in services can occur with an individual practitioner when that provider is not part of a new contract of care (Sharfstein, 1994). "Too often treatment is totally disrupted when a new group of providers is introduced in the middle of treatment for patients who already have a therapeutic alliance with their own practitioner. There are often intense issues related to abandonment that take on an ethical aspect" (Sharfstein, 1994, p. 197). In addition, since managed care companies control the purse strings of treatment, they have considerable power with regard to the continuity and continuation of service provisions.

Consider the following ethical dilemmas which may be encountered by social workers practicing in a managed care environment:

1. A social worker is authorized to see a client for eight sessions, but believes that the treatment will take significantly longer. Should the social worker see the client, perform a complete evaluation, and hope to get further authorization for treatment or refuse to treat the client based on the limitation of services?

2. After being in treatment for a little over a year, a client receives a letter from his/her managed care company stating that mental health benefits will be terminated after the next session with the social worker because the managed care company feels that length of treatment has been too long for the condition being treated. The client cannot afford to pay privately for services, but the social worker still feels that further treatment is warranted. After seeing the client free of charge for a while, the social worker finds that this pro bono service is causing financial hardship. However, the client cannot pay for mental health services and neither the social worker nor the client feel that transferring the client to another therapist is appropriate at this time. Should the social worker have to close his/her practice due to financial difficulties which have occurred for not being paid for his/her time? Will the close of the practice then place other clients at risk? Should the social worker place the client at risk by terminating therapy prematurely or referring him/her to another therapist?

3. During a therapy session, a client begins to bring to the surface issues which were not disclosed during the initial evaluation and are much more serious than the problem for which the client was initially referred by the managed care company. Due to the seriousness of the issues, the social worker believes that the client is going to be in need of continual treatment for an extended period of time. However, the social worker also knows that the client's managed care company is not likely to pay for continued treatment for as long as the client needs it. What should the social worker do?

All of these scenarios pose significant ethical dilemmas for social work practitioners. Simon (1994) suggests that the following preparation be taken by practitioners in order to avoid abandonment or interruption of services for clients.

1. The therapist must decide whether to even begin treatment of a patient whom he/she believes would be harmed by the brief treatment available.
2. The therapist must determine what other sources of treatment are available where the patient can be seen for little or no cost.
3. The therapist should prepare the patient by discussing other options prior to starting treatment.
4. The therapist should ask the patient to sign a form indicating that the specific limitations have been explained by the therapist and understood by the patient. (Simon, 1994, p. 124)

It is important to note that social workers must make every possible effort, including implementing the above mentioned preventative safeguards into their practices, in order to ensure that services to clients are not interrupted. However, the actions of the therapists must remain ethical and within the boundaries of their roles. Acceptable and appropriate actions include advocating with managed care companies, referring clients to other providers when clinically appropriate, or providing services at reduced or no costs whenever possible. NASW dictates that "when managed care organizations determine that they will no longer authorize payment for services by virtue of benefit limits, the social worker has the obligation to assure that appropriate services are made available to the client" (NASW, 1993, p. 10). The options include acceptance of private payment at a regular or reduced fee, pro bono services, or referral to alternative treatment sources. However, social workers must never misdiagnose clients or misrepresent the severity of clients' problems in order to gain authorization for more sessions. In addition, social workers must not discourage clients from discussing issues or concerns which need to be addressed in therapy even when it is known by them that it is likely that managed care will not pay for the extended treatment that is required. Instead, patients need to be informed of the limitations of their benefits and possible treatment options to address such problems.

In addition, social workers must never assume that policies of managed care companies are ethical as defined by their profession. By making such assumptions, social workers may violate established practice standards in one or more of the following areas: self-determination, informed consent, competence, conflicts of interest, privacy and confidentiality, and the interruption and termination of services. Social workers must remember that the policies of managed care companies represent competing, and often conflicting, interests such as cost containment and service quality. It is, therefore, not safe to believe that the interests of clients have always taken precedence in policy formation.

In order to assist them in resolving the many ethical dilemmas which are likely to arise from conflicts between social work practice standards and managed care company policies, social workers should put into place formal safeguards in addition to the informal ones previously mentioned. Formal safeguards include:

- *Establishing Peer Ethics Committees*–Peer ethics committees can serve as forums in which social work practitioners discuss and obtain guidance with regard to ethical conflicts encountered in daily practice. Since these committees are comprised of professionals who have had similar experiences and who are currently practicing within the field, social workers will feel free to share their experiences while possibly obtaining useful "real life" strategies for resolving dilemmas.
- *Developing Written Practice Guidelines for Managed Care*–Social work practitioners must develop written policies and procedures which outline their practice in the areas of client self-determination, informed consent, competence, conflicts of interest, privacy and confidentiality, and the interruption and termination of services. By outlining these practices in advance, social workers will not only have given careful forethought to these issues, but will be able to clearly articulate their protocols in these areas to both their clients and managed care companies. This forethought and clarity will greatly reduce the likelihood of ethical violations which usually result from quick decisions and vague guidelines. In addition, written policies can serve as the standards against which social workers monitor their own practices. Finally, written practice guidelines establish a uniformity of treatment with regard to these difficult issues, thereby reducing practices

which are discriminatory, based upon the whims of therapists, or those which deviate from the standards of the profession.

Given the recent growth of managed care, it is probable that most social workers will soon be delivering services within these networks if they are not already doing so. This will prove to be increasingly problematic for social workers as they attempt to uphold their ethical principals in a system which is focused on limiting spending. Given the potential inverse relationship between money spent on services and quality of care provided, it is also likely that social workers will be faced with ethical decisions and conflicts which go far beyond those for which their clinical training has prepared them. It is, therefore, essential that they adhere to the ethical standards of their profession as described in the newly revised Code of Ethics (NASW, 1996). In order to do so, social workers will need to engage in both micro- and macro-level practice as they advocate for their clients individually as well as promote systems changes which are in the best interest of clients overall. As more social workers continue to struggle with their dual commitment as providers of managed care for companies and quality care for clients, it is certain that additional training and practice guidelines in this area will be developed. Until then, however, social workers must forge ahead and take comfort in knowing that they are not alone as they individually wrestle with the ethical issues of their own clinical practices.

REFERENCES

Bak, J.S., Weiner, R.H., & Jackson, L.J. (1991). "Managed Mental Health Care: Should Independent Private Practitioners Capitate or Mobilize? (Part 2)." *The Texas Psychologist*, 43, 15-22.

Blum, S.R. (1992). "Ethical Issues in Managed Mental Health Care." in S. Feldman (Ed.), *Managed Mental Health Services* (pp. 245-265). Springfield, IL: Charles C. Thomas.

DeLeon, P.H., VandenBos, G.R., & Bulatao, E.Q. (1991). "Managed Mental Health Care: A History of the Federal Policy Initiative." *Professional Psychology: Research and Practice*, 22, 115-125.

Dow, M.M. (1993). *Managed Care Digest, Update Edition*. 3.

Elpers, J.R. & Abbott, B.K. (1992). "Public Policy, Ethical Issues, and Mental Health Administration." *Administration and Policy in Mental Health*, 19(6), 437-447.

Geraty, R.D., Hendren, R.L., & Flaa, C.J. (1992). "Ethical Perspectives on Managed

Care as It Relates to Child and Adolescent Psychiatry." *Journal of the American Academy of Child and Adolescent Psychiatry*, 31(3), 398-402.

Gottlieb, M.C. (1992). "Practicing Ethically with Managed-Care Patients." in L. VandeCreek, S. Knapp, & T. Jackson (Eds.), *Innovations in Clinical Practice: A Source Book* (Vol. II, pp. 481-493). Sarasota, FL: Professional Resource Press.

Haas, L. & Malouf, J. (1989). *Keeping up the Good Work: A Practitioner's Guide to Mental Health Ethics*. Sarasota, FL: Professional Resources Exchange, Inc.

National Association of Social Workers. (June 1993). *The Social Work Perspective on Managed Care for Mental Health and Substance Abuse Treatment*. Washington: DC: NASW.

National Association of Social Workers. (May 1994). *A Brief Look at Managed Mental Health Care*. Washington, DC: NASW.

National Association of Social Workers. (November 1996). *Code of Ethics*. Washington, DC: NASW.

Newman, R. & Brickman, P.M. (1991). "Parameters of Managed Mental Health Care: Legal, Ethical, and Professional Guidelines." *Professional Psychology: Research and Practice*, 22, 26-35.

Pope, K. & Vasquez, M. (1991). *Ethics in Counseling and Psychotherapy*. San Francisco, CA: Jossey-Bass.

Psychotherapy Finances. (October 1996). "Using Performance Incentives to Instill a Managed Care Sensibility in Clinical Staff." *Managed Care Strategies*, Jupiter, FL: Psychotherapy Finances.

Sabin, J.E. (1994). "Caring About Patients and Caring About Money: The American Psychiatric Association Code of Ethics Meets Managed Care." *Behavioral Sciences and the Law*, 12, 317-330.

Schreter, R.K., Sharfstein, S.S., & Schreter, C.A. (Eds.). (1994). *Allies and Adversaries: The Impact of Managed Care on Mental Health Services*. Washington, DC: American Psychiatric Press, Inc.

Sederer, L.I. & St.Clair, L. (1989). "Managed Health Care and the Massachusetts Experience." *American Journal of Psychiatry*, 146(9), 1142-1148.

Sharfstein, S.S. (1994). "Ethical Issues Under Managed Care." in R.H. Schreter, S.S. Sharfstein, & C.A. Schreter (Eds.), *Allies and Adversaries: The Impact of Managed Care on Mental Health Services* (pp. 195-200). Washington, DC: American Psychiatric Press, Inc.

Simon, N.P. (1994). "Ethics, Psychodynamic Treatment, and Managed Care." *Psychoanalysis & Psychotherapy*, 11(2), 119-128.

Stromberg, C.D., Haggarty, D.J., Liebenluft, R.F., McMillian, M.M., Mishkin, B., Rubin, B.L., & Trilling, H.R. (1988). *The Psychologist's Legal Handbook*. Washington, DC: The Council for the National Register of Health Service Providers in Psychology.

Effects of Confidentiality Law on Patient Self-Disclosure: Implications for the Therapeutic Relationship and Therapy Outcome

Marcia Kaufman, EdS, PhD (cand.)
Sandra S. Lee, PhD

SUMMARY. Confidentiality represents an important obligation to patients of mental health professionals. It typically invokes an explicit promise to reveal nothing about a patient without that individual's expressed, informed consent (McQuire, Toal, & Blau, 1985). The advent of the Tarasoff case has changed the scope of confidentiality both ethically and legally since the birth of the psychology profession. Consideration for the welfare of the individual patient was weighed against consideration for the welfare of society as a whole. How confidentiality law affects patients' self-disclosures, the therapeutic relationship, and ultimate therapy outcome is not yet clear. This paper explores the effects of confidentiality law on these issues. *[Article copies available for a fee from The*

Marcia Kaufman, EdS, is a PhD candidate at Seton Hall University, Department of Professional Psychology and Family Therapy. Her areas of interest include psychotherapy training and the therapeutic alliance.

Sandra S. Lee, PhD, Professor at Seton Hall University, Department of Professional Psychology and Family Therapy, teaches and writes in the areas of ethics and professional and training issues in psychology.

Address correspondence to: Marcia Kaufman, EdS, 4475 Farm Drive, Allentown, PA 18104 (E-Mail: Kaufmama@aol.com).

[Haworth co-indexing entry note]: "Effects of Confidentiality Law on Patient Self-Disclosure: Implications for the Therapeutic Relationship and Therapy Outcome." Kaufman, Marcia, and Sandra S. Lee. Co-published simultaneously in *Critical Strategies: Psychotherapy in Managed Care* (The Haworth Press, Inc.) Vol. 1, No. 1, 2000, pp. 105-120; and: *Psycho-Economics: Managed Care in Mental Health in the New Millennium* (ed: Robert D. Weitz) The Haworth Press, Inc., 2000, pp. 105-120. Single or multiple copies of this article are available for a fee from The Haworth Document Delivery Service [1-800-342-9678, 9:00 a.m. - 5:00 p.m. (EST). E-mail address: getinfo@haworthpressinc.com].

© 2000 by The Haworth Press, Inc. All rights reserved.

*Haworth Document Delivery Service: 1-800-342-9678. E-mail address: getinfo@
haworthpressinc.com <Website: http://www.haworthpressinc.com>]*

KEYWORDS. Confidentiality, confidentiality law, law, patient disclosure,
self-disclosure, lawtherapeutic alliance, managed care

Confidentiality represents an important obligation to patients of
mental health professionals. It invokes an explicit promise to reveal
nothing about a patient without that individual's expressed, informed
consent (McQuire, Toal, & Blau, 1985). The advent of the Tarasoff
case has changed the scope of confidentiality both ethically and legally since the birth of the psychology profession. When speaking of
"Confidentiality Law," it is the legal ramifications of this case which
are being referenced in this paper. With the Tarasoff court ruling, the
"protective privilege (confidentiality) ended where the public peril
began" (Bersoff, 1976, p. 268). Since Tarasoff professionals in the
field of psychotherapy have debated the merit of the case and the
potential cost to patients. There are still some psychotherapists who
feel that confidentiality is "sacred" and should be binding at all costs
(Siegel, 1976; Mangalmurti, 1994). There are other professionals who
believe that confidentiality should be breached in certain circumstances and this belief is expressed in the psychologist's professional
ethics (American Psychological Association, 1992; Mangalmurti,
1994).

How confidentiality law affects patients' self-disclosures, the therapeutic relationship, and ultimate therapy outcome is not yet clear.
Although some empirical research has been attempted in this area, the
results are mixed. This paper will explore the effects of confidentiality
law on patient self-disclosure, therapy alliance, and ultimate therapy
outcome. First, a history of confidentiality law will be presented,
including discussion of the Tarasoff case. Then, empirical research
which has examined the effects of confidentiality law on patients'
self-disclosures, therapist and patient feelings about confidentiality
law, and effects of informed consent on patients' self-disclosures will
be discussed. The therapeutic alliance, its components, its importance
in effecting therapy outcome and the role of self-disclosure in the
therapy relationship will then be analyzed. Finally, conclusions will be

drawn regarding the potential impact of confidentiality law on patient self-disclosure, therapy alliance, and ultimate therapy outcome.

HISTORY OF CONFIDENTIALITY
AND CONFIDENTIALITY LAW

The ethical professional duty of medical confidentiality can be traced to the Oath of Hippocrates, which states:

> What I see or hear in the course of treatment or even outside of the treatment in regard to the life of men, which on no account one must spread abroad, I will keep to myself holding such things shameful to be spoken about. (Mendelson & Mendelson, 1991, p. 38)

This oath obligated the physician to keep confidential all that he observed or became aware of during treatment and also required the doctor not to divulge any information gathered outside of his medical activity that related to his professional relationship with the patient (Mendelson & Mendelson, 1991).

The psychology profession also imposed this obligation on its practitioners (Siegel, 1976). For the psychologist, confidentiality consists of the ethical obligation protecting patients from unauthorized disclosures of information that are given in confidence, without consent (Miller & Thelen, 1986). However, unlike Hippocrates, modern day psychologists must consider circumstances which could result in clear danger to the patient or others when dealing with the issue of confidentiality. The newest Code of Ethics (American Psychological Association, 1992) mandates disclosure, if necessary without consent, in these circumstances. Changes in the psychologists' Code of Ethics occurred as a result of the 1974 Tarasoff case in which the California Supreme Court held that a therapist could be held liable for his breach of: "duty to use reasonable care to give threatened persons such warnings as are essential to avert foreseeable danger arising from his patient's condition and treatment" (Mendelson & Mendelson, 1991, p. 34).

In a dissenting opinion, Justice William Clark disagreed that the duty to warn should surpass confidentiality, stating that the threat of disclosure would greatly impair treatment (Kagel & Kopels, 1994). At the time, there were some psychotherapists who agreed with Justice Clark and felt that confidentiality is sacred and should be binding at all costs (Siegel, 1976; Mangalmurti, 1994). Max Siegel (1976), in his first Presidential Column for Division 12 of the American Psychological Association wrote: "Note, please, that I accept no conditions, no circumstances, under which confidentiality may be breached" (Siegel, 1976, p. 1).

In a rare occurrence, in 1976, the court reheard the Tarasoff case, and subsequently overturned the original ruling. The second ruling modified the first and instead of holding that therapists have a "simple duty to warn," the court held that the therapist must take reasonable steps to protect the safety of potential victims (Mangalmurti, 1994). While "reasonable steps" could invoke warning the victim, such a response is not necessarily the only one available (Mangalmurti, 1994). Subsequent to this ruling, different states have created different laws relating to this issue. Since the Tarasoff case was decided in California, its results have no binding legal effect in other states (Knapp & Tepper, 1996), thus each state has taken the Tarasoff precedent and created its own set of confidentiality laws (DeKraai & Sales, 1984; Monahan, 1993; Nowell & Spruill, 1993). Regardless of the particular state law, the "duty to protect" is in reality a fact of professional life for nearly all American clinicians and potentially, for clinical researchers as well (Monahan, 1993).

The impact of the Tarsoff ruling has modified therapists' views on the issue of confidentiality and when it should be breached. Data suggests that either as a result of Tarasoff or as a result of altered sensibilities, therapists may be more concerned about the threat to self and others in society and less zealous of patient confidentiality than they once were (Mangalmurti, 1994). In addition to altered beliefs, therapists' actions have changed as well, with twice as many therapists reporting to police since Tarasoff than before (Mangalmurti, 1994).

It appears that Tarasoff may have altered the face of psychotherapy. Therapists are more likely to divulge confidential information today than they were 20 years ago (Mangalmurti, 1994) and they seem to have lowered the threshold at which they consider a patient dangerous (Quinn, 1984). It appears that since Tarasoff the inviolability of the therapist-patient privilege has weakened (Mangalmurti, 1994). Empirical research has examined the effects of confidentiality law on patient self-disclosure, therapist and patient feelings about confidentiality, and effects of informed consent on patient self-disclosure. This empirical research will now be discussed.

EMPIRICAL RESEARCH ON EFFECTS
OF CONFIDENTIALITY LAW
ON PATIENT SELF-DISCLOSURE

Empirical research reports mixed results about the effects of confidentiality law on patient self-disclosure. Some studies have supported the conclusion that assurances of privacy have a minimal effect on encouraging disclosures, whereas others have supported the view that privacy is essential to encouraging openness in psychotherapy (Taube & Elwork, 1990). Woods and McNamara (1980) found that individuals receiving the promise of confidentiality were more open in their disclosures than those given nonconfidential instructions. Data was obtained by utilizing analogue situations with undergraduate students who were not from a clinical population. The authors suggest that their findings support the conclusion that the promise of confidentiality does make a difference, in an analogue therapy interview situation, in how open individuals are in their disclosures. "Clinical folklore and opinion suggest that when clients are assured of confidentiality of their communications, they will become less anxious and be more open about themselves" (Woods & McNamara, 1980, p. 720). The authors feel that their study supports clinical folklore and opinion. Gender differences were also noted in their results. In the confidential condition, disclosure was about the same for males and females. In the nonconfidential condition, however, females disclosed less than males. Results from this and other studies indicate that the possible release of confidential information is less negatively valued by males than by females (Woods & McNamara, 1980).

Taube and Elwork (1990) hypothesized that conflicting research findings on the effects that confidentiality laws have on patients' self-disclosures reflect the fact that privacy is important only to some patients in some circumstances. They found that self-disclosures about sensitive issues such as child abuse and drug abuse during intake were determined partly by how legally informed patients were and partly by how relevant and consequential the law was to their cases. Their findings support the hypothesis that current limitations of confidentiality in psychotherapy matter only to some patients in some circumstances. The authors feel that the most important implication of their study is that the legal and ethical debate on the limits to confidentiality needs to get beyond the issue of whether current law has a generally negative effect on psychotherapy. Instead, they suggest, policymakers and researchers should begin to determine precisely when and how confidentiality limits affect therapy or prevent harm. Study results furthermore suggest that laws that limit privacy of particular types of "confessions" may discourage certain patients from being candid in the first place. As a result, these laws may fail to achieve their goal of protecting society while they may also hinder treatment (Taube & Elwork, 1990).

McQuire et al. (1985) assessed clients' understanding/valuing of confidentiality and privilege in the therapeutic relationship. Results revealed that subjects significantly valued confidentiality. They also revealed that clients were generally unable to differentiate between privacy as an ethical versus a legal concept. Outpatients who perceived violations in their privacy in past or current counseling tended to place lower value on issues with confidentiality than did subjects who reported no violation of confidences within a counseling relationship. The investigators report that their findings are consistent with previous investigators and suggest that mental health clients both value and expect that their communications with a counselor will generally be held in confidence. The investigators were alarmed to find that many clients perceived that the privacy of their counseling relationship had been significantly compromised. They felt that this perception had a significantly negative impact on the overall valuing of the concept of privacy in counseling. The authors suggest that the potential implications of these findings for the establishment of trust in the counselor and the willingness of the client to disclose personal information critical to the intra/interpersonal learning process is apparent. They suggest the need for increased pretreatment discussion of the meaning and limitations of confidentiality, which speaks to the issue of informed consent.

Kobocow, McGuire, and Blau (1983) assessed the effects of varying degrees of assurance of confidentiality on frequency of self-disclosure in a junior high school population. The principal hypothesis of the study stated that the frequency of self-disclosure of personal information would be greatest under conditions of explicit assurances of confidentiality and lowest under conditions of explicit lack of confidentiality. The results of the study did not support this main hypothesis. However, mean disclosure scores to questions rated most sensitive for both male and female subjects were higher under conditions of explicit confidentiality than nonconfidentiality. Across conditions, males were seen to disclose more than females. These gender findings are similar to findings in the Woods and McNamara (1980) study. Study investigators felt the results may have occurred because people assumed confidentiality even when it was not explicitly promised. This assumption was based on the fact that there was a highly significant overoccurrence of recall of confidentiality instructions and a disproportionate underreporting of nonconfidential and neutral instructions.

Empirical research has also explored therapist and patient feelings about confidentiality and its limitations. Jagim, Wittman, and Noll (1978) surveyed mental health professionals in North Dakota about their knowledge and attitudes toward three important ethical-legal issues: confidentiality, privilege, and disclosure of information to third parties. The survey results demonstrated agreement on the importance of confidentiality in the therapeutic relationship. Furthermore, the results suggested the need for clients to be informed about the conditions under which exceptions to the general principle of confidentiality would occur.

Miller and Thelen (1986) conducted a survey to assess the public's knowledge and attitudes regarding confidentiality of therapeutic communications. The public responded in the following ways: 69% of respondents believed that everything discussed in the context of psychotherapy is considered confidential by psychotherapists; 74% maintained there should be no exceptions to the proposition that all information should be confidential; 96% desired to be apprised of information pertaining to confidentiality; and 45% desired to be told of exceptions to confidentiality before the first session. The investigators concluded that the general population does not have an accurate perception of current ethical limitations regarding the confidentiality of information discussed in psychotherapy. In writing their concluding remarks, the authors discuss the psychotherapists' dilemma. Their findings indicated that most people view confidentiality as an all-encompassing, superordinate mandate for the profession of psychology. In addition, their survey indicated that the public desires to be told of the limits of confidentiality, and yet when told, people may not subsequently participate in psychotherapy. Hence, Miller and Thelen (1986) write: "the clinician is thrust between Charybdis and Scylla" (p. 18).

VandeCreek, Miars, and Herzog (1987) surveyed new clients requesting services at a university counseling center. They asked clients to rate the amount of information that they preferred and anticipated would be released by their psychotherapist under 13 request scenarios. In general, clients preferred less information to be released than they anticipated would be, but differences existed by scenario and recipient. Some clients preferred absolute confidentiality, while others preferred broader releases of information. The individuality of responses is consistent with the work of Taube and Elwork (1990), which has previously been discussed. The investigators felt that their results indicate that clients clearly value confidentiality in counseling since the majority of clients preferred that their counselor reveal little information to others.

Informed consent has been alluded to in the discussion of empirical research in the area of confidentiality. The Ethical Principles of Psychologists and Code of Conduct (American Psychological Association, 1992) speaks to this issue and discusses the limits of confidentiality with patients. Muehleman, Pickens, and Robinson (1985) investigated the effects of providing varying amounts of detail regarding the limits to confidentiality in a psychology analogue. Little evidence emerged of significant inhibition of disclosure when detailed information was provided. The authors view their results as encouraging to psychologists concerned about the moral rights of their clients as well as to psychologists who have avoided informing clients about the limits to confidentiality. As can be seen from the Ethical Principles of Psychologists and Code of Conduct (American Psychological Association, 1992) however, psychologists are mandated to inform their clients of limits to confidentiality. The investigators concluded from the results of their study that providing detailed information about the limits to confidentiality probably will not inhibit relevant patient self-disclosure in the therapeutic setting. They hypothesized in their conclusion that an interview atmosphere conducive to trust and self-exploration and the patient's motivation for seeking help may be the overriding factors determining self-disclosure. The authors did find, however, that offering complete confidentiality, as compared to nearly total lack of confidentiality, does make a difference in disclosure in a group setting.

Dauser, Hedstrom, and Croteau (1995) also found that offering pretherapy information does not lead to negative effects in therapy. Rights and limits of confidentiality was one of 12 types of information disclosed to subjects. Although both the control and experimental groups received confidentiality information, that this study found no negative effects resulting from written pretherapy disclosure is significant.

Haut and Muehleman (1986) found that when limits to confidentiality were conveyed in a clear and specific manner there was no decrease in self-disclosure. Contrary to the findings of Haut and Muehleman however, clinical psychologists surveyed in the same study incorrectly predicted that increasing clarity and specificity of information concerning the limits to confidentiality would lead to decreased disclosure by interviewees. In this study, single mothers were assigned to either a reference group or one of three groups that received an informed consent form prior to a clinical interview. The forms differed in the amount of specificity and clarity of information pertaining to the limits to confidentiality. While their investigation found no evidence that there was a difference in disclosure when the limits to confidentiality were more specifically conveyed, subjects who received information concerning the limits to confidentiality disclosed less information that the subjects who presumed anonymity (reference group). The condition in which persons could report discipline practices in private and with anonymity promised led to more disclosure of "severe" discipline practices than within the interview situation. The psychologists' Code of Ethics and the confidentiality laws preclude the option of promising total confidentiality under these circumstances, however. The question raised for practicing psychotherapists is whether or not to take a position of absolute confidentiality in an effort to obtain a higher level of client disclosure (Haut & Muehleman, 1986). Taking this position places the therapist in a position where conflict with both the law and the professional ethics is certain. The study investigators feel that "if the loss in disclosure exists, it may be possible to overcome this through basic clinical skills such as empathy and understanding" (p. 101). Given the current legal and ethical climate, this certainly appears to be the therapist's only option.

In a study which examined why clients relinquish their rights to privacy under sign-away pressures, Rosen (1977) found that clients will sign release of information forms when they think they have to in order to get services. When clients were told they had a choice of whether or not to sign the forms, only 41% of clients complied and signed the forms. In a clinic where one group of clients heard they had no choice, all signed the forms. With the group who was told there was an option, only 20% signed. Again, given the current legal and ethical climate, psychotherapists are unable to offer their clients the choice of total confidentiality. The results of the Rosen (1977) study raise questions regarding choices clients would make if they, in fact, did have the option of carte blanche confidentiality.

One of the reasons given for nonexceptions to confidentiality is the negative impact it will have on the therapeutic relationship (Miller & Thelen, 1986; Siegel, 1976). When the public was questioned in an open-response format regarding confidentiality, 75% of all respondents felt that confidentiality was maintained in therapy in order to facilitate the therapeutic relationship (Miller & Thelen, 1986). The therapeutic relationship, or therapeutic alliance, its components, and its importance in effecting therapy outcome will now be explored. Self-disclosure in relation to the therapeutic alliance will also be discussed.

THE THERAPEUTIC ALLIANCE, ITS EFFECT ON THERAPY OUTCOME AND THE ROLE OF SELF-DISCLOSURE

The therapeutic alliance can be defined as "the observable ability of the therapist and patient to work together in a realistic, collaborative relationship based on mutual respect, liking, trust and commitment to the work of treatment" (Klee, Abeles, & Muller, 1990, p. 166). For some, the alliance is viewed as a mechanism for change, and for others it is viewed as a mechanism that enables the patient to comply with treatment (Sexton & Whitson, 1994). However it is viewed, the therapeutic relationship is multifaceted and complex, and empirical research supports that this complex component of therapy is most predictive of outcome (Horvath & Symonds, 1991; Sexton & Whitson, 1994). In fact, recent research in the area of the therapeutic alliance indicates that it might account for up to 45% of the variance in measurable outcome (Gaston, 1990; Sexton & Whitson, 1994).

Although much of the theoretical and empirical work on the therapeutic alliance has primarily come from psychodynamic and client-centered traditions, there has recently been a growing recognition of the role of the alliance in other psychotherapy approaches, such as cognitive and behavior therapy. Even in pharmacotherapy, the importance of the alliance has been postulated as a factor influencing compliance, and therefore outcome (Gaston, 1990). Many factors have been studied which have been suspected of influencing the therapeutic alliance. Length of treatment, therapist and patient factors, and therapist interventions have all been empirically investigated (Horvath, Gaston, & Luborsky, 1993; Horvath & Luborsky, 1993; Horvath & Symonds, 1991; Sexton & Whitson, 1994). The clinical literature has explored the roles of transference, countertransference, resistance, and counterresistance in the therapy relationship.

In the psychotherapeutic process, self-disclosure promotes intimacy, which allows therapy to proceed. Self-disclosure has even been found to be therapeutic in and of itself. Research over the past decade indicates that talking or even writing about emotions or personal upheavals can boost autonomic nervous system activity, immune function, and physical health (Pennebaker, 1995). Healey (1990) wrote that there are two important elements, two necessary preconditions, before self-disclosure can take place. The first condition is a relationship and the second is trust. Self-disclosure can be defined, somewhat tautologically, as a process by which the self is revealed (Stricker, 1990). In order for self-disclosure to occur, there must be a person who self-discloses and a person who receives the self-disclosure. When the discloser is the patient and the receiver is the therapist, the therapist serves a self-regulatory function, aiding the patient in developing a clearer sense of the meaning and import of the self-disclosure (Stricker, 1990). The patient may resist self-disclosing, for to do so may mean rediscovering a disavowed portion of himself or herself. In other words, the essential secrets may not be kept from the therapist, but from the self (Stricker, 1990). The therapist is merely a conduit who encourages and allows the patient to explore ideas, risk disclosures, and come to understand that these secrets are not destructive, can be tolerated by others, and perhaps can be tolerated by the self (Stricker, 1990). How does confidentiality law influence self-disclosure under these circumstances? If therapists are to encourage patients to risk disclosures and come to understand that these secrets are not destructive, can be tolerated by others and perhaps tolerated by the self how do confidentiality limits promote these processes?

Freud felt that the patient needs a safe environment for personal self-disclosure, including reassurances that his or her communications will be confidential and no punishment will result from saying whatever comes to mind (Lane & Hull, 1990). Cornerstones of psychoanalytic inquiry include explorations of patient anxiety, transference, and resistance. "Under the impetus of anxiety, the patient often utilizes the transference in order to act out the resistance" (Fisher, 1990, p. 4). In like fashion, this experience of the patient is often met by the counter-anxiety, the countertransference, and the counterresistance of the therapist. What then takes place in the arena of psychotherapy is inextricably woven and interwoven in a combined interaction between patient and therapist. Who is influencing whom, at any given moment, and in what direction, to what end, is a function of that interaction (Fisher, 1990). This is what may be referred to as the psychotherapy of "shared experience" (Fisher, 1990). Sullivan used the term "collaboration" and described it as a mutually rewarding relationship that promotes a reciprocal validation and personal worth. The therapeutic dyad has been described as being of limited value unless implemented within a relationship characterized by an effectional bond of mutual trust and respect (Fisher, 1990). When considering the impact of confidentiality law on self-disclosure, these processes must not be overlooked. Resistance on the part of the patient may evoke countertransferential feelings and resistances in the therapist. Implications for treatment are vast, as reluctance to self-disclose on the patient's part may be spurred on by knowledge of confidentiality limits.

Psychotherapy is based on the patient talking to the therapist; on the patient's self-disclosure. But, will the patient self-disclose if in that chance-taking he or she will be humiliated, rejected, or still worse destroyed (Fisher, 1990)? Does limiting confidentiality compromise the patient's willingness to say everything in an effort to be healed? Does limiting confidentiality influence the therapeutic relationship and ultimately therapy outcome? Does limiting confidentiality promote cure?

CONCLUSION

Research has explored the effects of confidentiality law on patients' self-disclosures and interviewee's behavior (Kobocow et al., 1983; McGuire et al., 1985; Taube & Elwork, 1990; Woods & McNamara, 1980), both in analogue and natural situations. Therapist and patient feelings about confidentiality law have also been investigated (Jagim et al., 1978; Miller & Thelen, 1986; VandeCreek et al., 1987). In addition, informed consent has been studied in terms of its effects on patient self-disclosure (Muehleman et al., 1985). In general it appears that although patients would prefer carte blanche confidentiality, they are accepting of the limits imposed by the law and appreciate being briefed on these limits through informed consent. As Mangalmurti (1994) states: "Therapy has not crumbled under the weight of Tarasoff" (p. 403).

However, the verdict is certainly not in on the effects of confidentiality law on patient self-disclosure and the implications for the therapeutic relationship and ultimate therapy outcome. There appear to be individual differences in the response to confidentiality limits. For example, research has indicated that females may be more guarded in their self-disclosures under these circumstances (Rosen, 1977; Vande-Creek et al., 1987; Woods & McNamara, 1980). Within the therapeutic relationship issues of transference, countertransference, resistance, and counterresistance may all be affected by limiting confidentiality. Since the therapeutic relationship has been found to be predictive of therapy outcome, confidentiality law has the potential of affecting therapy outcome as well; the questions are how, for whom, and under what circumstances.

"The essence of psychotherapy is a specialized human relationship designed to mediate an experience that brings about constructive changes in the patient's self-concept and behavior" (Strupp & Binder, 1984, p. 40). The therapist, as a professional, is a trained clinical observer whose expertise is encompassed by an ability to understand the nature of the patient's difficulties and to turn this understanding to therapeutic advantage (Strupp & Binder, 1984). Prior to Tarasoff confidentiality was a given in an effort to promote patient self-disclosure and work toward patient cure. The advent of the Tarasoff case changed the scope of confidentiality both ethically and legally. As the potential effects of this case are assessed, consideration for the welfare of the individual patient is weighed against consideration for the welfare of society as a whole. Although the intent of Tarasoff and the resulting confidentiality laws is to protect society, does limiting confidentiality do just that? Some would argue that if patients are less comfortable disclosing their violent and self-destructive thoughts, they may be more apt to act rather than to talk (Mangalmurti, 1994). Perhaps, if patients are resistant to rediscovering the disavowed portions of themselves in the first place, their resistance may only be intensified by their knowledge of confidentiality limits. Thus, the process of psychotherapy may be compromised and the very laws that intend to protect society may do it more harm than good.

The current ethical and legal climate promotes the idea that absolute confidentiality, and the promise of absolute confidentiality, may reflect a lack of societal responsibility (Miller & Thelen, 1986). However, prudent therapists should consider the potential impact of the confidentiality law on patient self-disclosure, therapy alliance, and ultimate therapy outcome. The impact may be greater and graver than previously thought. Perhaps, in an effort to protect patients and society, both are left unprotected because there is not safety and freedom to say everything. Patients may then feel that the only thing left to do may be to act.

REFERENCES

American Psychological Association. (1992). *Ethical principles of psychologists and code of conduct. Washington, D.C.: Author.*

Bersoff D. (1976). Therapists as protectors and policemen: New roles as a result of Tarasoff. *Professional Psychology*, 267-273.

Dauser, P., Hedstrom, S., & Croteau, J. (1995). Effects of disclosure on comprehensive pretherapy information on clients at a university counseling center. *Professional Psychology: Research and Practice, 26*, 190-195.

DeKraai, M. & Sales, B. (1984). Confidential communications of psychotherapists. *Psychotherapy, 21*, 293-318.

Fisher, M. (1990). The shared experience and self-disclosure. In G. Stricker & M. Fisher (Eds.), *Self-disclosure in the therapeutic relationship* (pp. 3-15). New York: Plenum Press.

Gaston, L. (1990). The concept of the alliance and its role in psychotherapy: theoretical and empirical considerations. *Psychotherapy, 27*, 143-153.

Haut, M. & Muehleman, T. (1986). Informed consent: The effects of clarity and specificity on disclosure in a clinical interview. *Psychotherapy, 23*, 293-318.

Healey, B. (1990). Self-disclosure in religious spiritual direction. In G. Stricker & M. Fisher (Eds.), *Self-disclosure in the therapeutic relationship* (pp. 17-30). New York: Plenum Press.

Horvath, A., Gaston, L., & Luborsky, L. (1993). The therapeutic alliance and its measures. In N. Miller, L. Luborsky, J. Barber, & J. Docherty (Eds.), *Psychodynamic treatment research* (pp. 247-273). New York: Basic Books.

Horvath, A. & Luborsky, L. (1993). The role of the therapeutic alliance in psychotherapy. *Journal of Consulting and Clinical Psychology, 61*, 561-573.

Horvath, A. & Symonds, D. (1991). Relation between working alliance and outcome in psychotherapy: A meta-analysis. *Journal of Counseling Psychology, 38*, 139-149.

Jagim, R, Wittman, W., & Noll, J. (1978). Mental health professionals' attitudes toward confidentiality, privilege, and third party disclosure. *Professional Psychology, 9*, 458-466.

Kagel, D. & Kopels, S. (1994). Confidentiality alter Tarasoff. *National Association of Social Workers, 19,* 217-222.

Klee, M., Abeles, N., & Muller, R (1990). Therapeutic alliance: Early indicators, course, and outcome. *Psychotherapy, 27,* 166-174.

Knapp, S. & Tepper, A. (1996). The duty to protect: What is its status in Pennsylvania? *The Pennsylvania Psychologist Quarterly, 56,* 24-25.

Kobocow, B., McQuire, J., & Blau, B. (1983). The influence of confidentiality conditions on self-disclosure of early adolescents. *Professional Psychology: Research and Practice, 14,* 435-443.

Lane, R & Hull, J. (1990). Self-disclosure and classical psychoanalysis. In G. Stricker & M. Fisher (Eds.), *Self-disclosure in the therapeutic relationship* (pp. 31-46). New York: Plenum Press.

Mangalmurti, V. (1994). Psychotherapists' fear of Tarasoff: All in the mind? *The Journal of Psychiatry and Law, 22,* 379-409.

McQuire, J., Toal, P., & Blau, B. (1985). The adult client's conception of confidentiality in the therapeutic relationship. *Professional Psychology: Research and Practice, 16,* 375-384.

Mendelson, D. & Mendelson, G. (1991). Tarasoff down under: The Psychiatrist's duty to warn in Australia. *The Journal of Psychiatry and Law, 19,* 33-61.

Miller, D. & Thelen, M. (1986). Knowledge and beliefs about confidentiality in psychotherapy. *Professional Psychology: Research and Practice, 17,* 15-19.

Monahan, J. (1993). Limiting therapist exposure to Tarasoff liability. *American Psychologist, 48,* 242-250.

Muehleman, T., Pickens, B., & Robinson, F. (1985). Informing clients about the limits to confidentiality, risks, and their rights: Is self-disclosure inhibited? *Professional Psychology: Research and Practice, 16,* 385-397.

Nowell, D. & Spruill, J. (1993). If it's not absolutely confidential will information be disclosed? *Professional Psychology: Research and Practice, 24,* 367-369.

Pennebaker, J. (1995). Emotion, disclosure, and health: An overview. In J. Pennebaker (Ed.), *Emotion, disclosure, and health* (pp. 3-10). Washington, D.C.: American Psychological Association.

Quinn, K (1984). The impact of Tarasoff on clinical practice. *Behavioral Sciences and the Law, 2,* 319-329.

Rosen, C. (1977). Why clients relinquish their rights to privacy under sign-away pressures. *Professional Psychology,* 17-24.

Sexton, T. & Whitson, S. (1994). The status of the counseling relationship: An empirical review, theoretical implications, and research directions. *The Counseling Psychologist, 22,* 6-78.

Siegel, M. (1976). Confidentiality. *The Clinical Psychologist, 30,* 1.

Stricker, G. (1990). Self-disclosure and psychotherapy. In G. Stricker & M. Fisher (Eds.), *Self-disclosure in the therapeutic relationship* (pp. 277-289). New York: Plenum Press.

Strupp, H. & Binder, J. (1984). *Psychotherapy in a new key.* New York: Basic Books.

Taube, D. & Elwork, A. (1990). Researching the effects of confidentiality law on patients' self-disclosures. *Professional Psychology: Research and Practice, 21,* 72-75.

VandeCreek, L., Miars, R, & Herzog, C. (1987). Client anticipations and preferences for confidentiality of records. *Journal of Counseling Psychology, 34*, 62-67.

Woods, K. & McNamara, R. (1980). Confidentiality: Its effect on interviewee behavior. *Professional Psychology, 11*, 714-721.

Why Clinical Social Workers
Decline Private Practice

Robert Seiz, PhD, CSW-ACP, BCD

SUMMARY. A random survey of social workers licensed in Texas at the advanced clinical practitioner level using self-administered questionnaires reveals the reasons–especially those the respondents deem most important–why experienced and eligible clinical social workers eschew a private practice. The overwhelming majority decline for reasons other than a restricted professional ideology. Comparisons are drawn between the reasons for declining a private practice and the reasons of part-time private practitioners for declining a full-time private practice. Implications for agency-based practice and for the growth trend in private practice in the era of managed care are explored. Four hundred twenty responses provide the data for this study. *[Article copies available for a fee from The Haworth Document Delivery Service: 1-800-342-9678. E-mail address: getinfo@haworthpressinc.com <Website: http://www.haworthpressinc. com>]*

KEYWORDS. Managed care, social work, private practice, independent practice

Despite its formal sanctioning over forty-one years ago in 1956 by the National Association of Social Workers, the private practice of social work remains a practice option mired in a larger controversy about social work's mission and visions of practice (Abramovitz,

Robert Seiz is affiliated with the Department of Social Work, Colorado State University, 127 Education, Fort Collins, CO 80523-1586 (E-mail: seiz@cahs.colostate.edu).

[Haworth co-indexing entry note]: "Why Clinical Social Workers Decline Private Practice." Seiz, Robert. Co-published simultaneously in *Critical Strategies: Psychotherapy in Managed Care* (The Haworth Press, Inc.) Vol. 1, No. 1, 2000, pp. 121-134; and: *Psycho-Economics: Managed Care in Mental Health in the New Millennium* (ed: Robert D. Weitz) The Haworth Press, Inc., 2000, pp. 121-134. Single or multiple copies of this article are available for a fee from The Haworth Document Delivery Service [1-800-342-9678, 9:00 a.m. - 5:00 p.m. (EST). E-mail address: getinfo@haworthpressinc.com].

121

1998; Haynes, 1998; Austin, 1997). Distinguished members of the social work profession can still be heard at conferences and in the professional journals asserting, or at least strongly implying, that private practitioners are not *really* social workers. For decades the curriculum committees of graduate social work programs refused to acknowledge the legitimacy of private practice and systematically excluded from the curriculum knowledge that would specifically prepare students for private practice (Brown & Barker, 1995). Of the numerous debates within social work, few have lasted as long as the dispute over private practice (Levenstein, 1964).

Those opposed to private practice contend that the ethos and vitality of the profession have been fundamentally, and perhaps fatally, fouled by the burgeoning numbers of social work psychotherapists and private practitioners–the late millennial equivalents of the Visigoth hordes that cracked Rome's walls (Specht, 1991; Waltz & Groze, 1991; Specht & Courtney, 1994; McNeece, 1995; Richey & Stevens, 1992; Ehrenreich, 1985; Trattner, 1994). Proponents counter that private practice is an important alternative form of service delivery for social workers who are dissatisfied with the bureaucratic restrictions, the inadequate direct practice opportunities, and the limited financial rewards associated with agency practice (Barker, 1991; Wakefield, 1992; Swenson, 1995). While much is known about social workers in private practice, and about their motivations, less is known about the reasons why social workers who are qualified by licensure and experience decline to engage in private practice (Strom, 1994b). It is unclear whether clinical social workers decline out of a belief that private practice is not consistent with the mission and practice of social work, or whether non-ideological concerns are more potent and prevalent in their reasoning and decisions to eschew private practice.

A GROWTH INDUSTRY

The private practice of social work has grown dramatically from very modest beginnings in the opening decades of the 20th century (Ehrenreich, 1985; Trattner, 1994). Levenstein (1964) estimated that through the early 1960s the number of social workers entering private practice had doubled every five years since 1925. In an unpublished paper, Sheafor and his associates (1998) present a preliminary analysis of national data collected in the mid-1990s from a stratified random sample of 4,266 MSWs drawn from the NASW membership list. Almost 25 percent of the respondents claimed private practice as an employment setting. This represents a substantial movement of social workers into private practice over the last 12 to 13 years, growing from 8.7 percent in 1984 to 24.5 percent in 1997.

Some link the growth of private practice to historical shifts in the relative attention social work places on the public versus the private. Franklin (1990) sees these shifts as cyclical, with discernable historical periods of ascendancy for each. She suggests that the growth of private practice is linked with the periods dominated by an emphasis on the private. Wagner (1989), however, suggests that the shifts are not real cycles, but are more properly to be seen as scant and short-lived detours from the relatively constant dominance of the private over the public. He views any shifts to the public as brief interruptions in the profession's preference for the private; a preference epitomized by the embrace of private practice by so many social workers. Other commentators contend that social work's professional associations facilitated and actively promoted the growth and expansion of private practice. The associations did this through their extensive investments of effort and financial resources towards obtaining clinical social work licensure in 52 states and jurisdictions, towards establishing vendorship eligibility or third-party payments for clinical social workers, and by advancing clinical social work credentialing through peer review and examination (Biggerstaff, 1995; Timberlake, Sabatino & Martin, 1997).

Whatever the reasons and whatever the forces, the fact remains that the growth trend in private practice has persisted and even accelerated. No one knows for sure exactly how many social workers are in private practice; but the numbers are certainly greater than the NASW data indicates since not all private practitioners are members of NASW. The consistent movement of clinical social workers into private practice produced profound and far-reaching changes in the profession (Gibelman & Schervish, 1996) and raised concerns about the future availability and quality of experienced clinicians in agency practice (Barker, 1992; Richey & Stevens, 1992).

PRIOR RESEARCH

The social work profession responded to the swelling numbers of private practitioners with an expanding collection of studies scrutinizing the phenomenon from a variety of perspectives. Studies investigated the historical development of private practice, (Levinstein, 1964; Barker, 1991; Cohen, 1966a); the personal profiles and professional practices of private practitioners (Timberlake, Sabatino & Martin, 1997; Strom, 1994a; Brown, 1991); their personality traits (Seiz & Schwab, 1992a); their levels of identification with the social work profession (Perlman, 1994); their motivations and aspirations (Alexander, 1987; Cohen, 1966b; Smaller, 1987; Saxton, 1988; Karger & Stoesz, 1994; Butler, 1992); their value systems (Seiz & Schwab, 1992b); their career paths into private practice (Cohen, 1966a; Giberlman & Schervish, 1993; 1996); their differences and similarities with their colleagues in agency-based practice (Jayaratne, Siefert & Chess, 1988; Borenzweig, 1981) and with psychologists in private practice (FitzPatrick & Pardeck, 1995); and the confluence of environmental forces, both within and outside the social work profession, affecting the expansion of private practice (Abramovitz, 1998 & 1986; Saxton, 1988; Jayaratne, Davis-Sacks & Chess, 1991; Karger & Stoesz, 1994; Strom, 1996; Goldstein, 1996).

Yet little is known of the reasons clinical social workers have for declining a private practice, and which reasons are most salient. Also unknown is whether the reasons given for not engaging in any private practice are different from the reasons offered by part-time private practitioners for not engaging in full-time private practice.

METHOD

To address these questions, an ex post facto study was designed that used a mail survey instrument that collected relevant data in five general areas: (1) demographic information on two groups of clinicians–those not in private practice and those in part-time private practice; (2) the reasons-including the most important ones–for declining a private practice; (3) the likelihood of engaging in private practice within the next five years; (4) the reasons–including the most important ones–for choosing part-time rather than full-time private practice; and, (5) the likelihood of engaging in full-time private practice within five years.

The self-administered questionnaire was mailed to 1,218 social workers in Texas who held an Advanced Clinical Practitioner license. This license requires an MSW, 3 years of post-MSW practice experience of which 2 must be under clinical supervision, and a passing score on the appropriate state examination. Social workers licensed at this level were targeted in order to control for education, identification with social work, and the length and nature of post-graduate professional social work experience. Except for unique circumstances, only social workers licensed at the Advanced Clinical Practitioner level can have an independent clinical private practice in Texas. While not specifically addressed in the questionnaire, it is reasonable to assume that, unlike similar studies, the study population was not limited to members of NASW, but was more representative of the larger population of social workers in Texas.

The placement of individuals into the comparison groups was determined by responses to the question: "In what social work setting are you currently working?" The response choices of interest to this study were: (1) "*agency only*," and (2) "*agency AND private practice.*" The issue of differentiating part-time from full-time private practice according to an arbitrary number of hours spent in private practice was avoided by using this self-classification system. It can be reasonably assumed that respondents who self-selected the "*agency and private practice*" response have a part-time private practice. Private practice was defined as "autonomous, for-profit social work practice that provides individual, couple, family, and/or group counseling or psychotherapy."

The mailing, with a general follow-up reminder by post card, resulted in a return rate of 52.7 percent (642 usable responses) which is considered adequate (Rubin & Babbie, 1993). Of the 642 respondents, 268 listed themselves as practicing in an agency only (no private practice) and 155 as practicing in an agency and in a private practice (i.e., had a part-time private practice). The remaining 219 had a full-time private practice and were not included in the data reported here.

The initial draft of the instrument was pre-tested for clarity and face validity using a voluntary sample of 12 similarly licensed clinical social workers. The possibility of respondent error in questionnaire interpretation and patterned response was controlled through questionnaire design and pre-testing. Data entry error was minimized through ongoing verification of the data by entering the data set twice and cross-checking for discrepancies. Sampling error was reduced through the use of an inclusive sampling frame, with final sample selection achieved by computer generated randomization. However, the almost

53 percent response rate, while not atypical for research using mailed surveys, leaves uncontrolled the possibility for an indeterminate degree of sampling error. Furthermore, the results may be influenced by the nature of self-report measures (Rubin & Babbie, 1993). Since the sample was limited to Texas, the study's findings cannot be generalized without additional research being conducted in other states to determine whether similar reasons and likelihoods exist. Likewise, the ideological positions of non-clinical social workers regarding the appropriateness or non-appropriateness of private practice to social work cannot be inferred and remain unknown. One may legitimately wonder whether non-clinical social workers as a group would share the perspectives of the clinical social workers in this study.

FINDINGS

Demographic Characteristics

On gender and ethnicity the respondents who returned questionnaires did not differ significantly from the population of all social workers licensed as Advanced Clinical Practitioners. Data on marital status, age, and locale of practice for the entire population were not available. Table 1 presents group breakouts by age, ethnicity, gender, marital status, and locale of practice. Differences in the number of respondents among categories result from incomplete responses. A concession to foreswear data analysis by demographic characteristics was taken in order to use as much data as reliably available to address the study's central research questions. Comparisons are presented for descriptive purposes only and significance cannot be inferred.

Reasons for Declining Private Practice

Clinical social workers cite many different reasons for declining to engage in a private practice. They generally have more than one reason. The dominant reasons have more to do with the practical demands and requirements of a private practice, factors that seem to serve as formidable hurdles and deterrents for many. Most who decline do so because they find private practice too risky, because it requires specific skills they do not possess, demands time they either don't have or are unwilling to devote, and is out of reach because of the absence of opportunities or the lack of support.

TABLE 1. Demographic Characteristics of Respondents

	Non-Private Practitioners		Part-Time Practitioners	
	N	Percent	N	Percent
Age				
Under 30	0	00.0%	0	00.0%
30-39	76	28.5%	39	25.4%
40-49	116	43.4%	69	45.0%
50+	75	28.1%	45	29.4%
Totals	199	100%	153	100%
Ethnicity				
Black	13	4.9%	4	2.6%
Hispanic	25	9.4%	14	9.25%
White	216	80.9%	126	82.4%
Other	13	4.9%	9	5.9%
Totals	267	100%	153	100%
Gender				
Female	174	65.7%	104	68.0%
Male	91	34.3%	49	32.0%
Totals	265	100%	153	100%
Marital Status				
Single	60	22.8%	31	20.5%
Married	175	66.5%	100	66.2%
S-H-Household	28	10.6%	20	13.2%
Totals	263	100%	151	100%
Community				
Urban	195	73.0%	108	70.1%
Suburban	28	10.5%	15	9.7%
Rural	11	4.1%	9	5.8%
Small Town	33	12.4%	22	14.3%
Totals	267	100%	154	100%

As Table 2 reveals, only a small subset (2.6 percent) cite the belief that the private practice of psychotherapy is not social work as the most important reason for declining private practice. The most frequently cited important reason(s) fell into the "other" category (31.5 percent). Examples offered by respondents to clarify what they meant in choosing this category included such comments as: "just not interested," "have to give up too much family time," "increased liability," "restraints placed by managed care," "private practice is too lonely" or "too emotionally intensive," and doing psychotherapy is "boring," "inefficient," or "requires psychiatric back-up."

One may wonder how many of these respondents might consider engaging in private practice sometime in the future. To address this question, respondents were asked to estimate, on a scale of 1 to 7

TABLE 2. Reasons for Declining Private Practice

	All Reasons *		Most Important Reason	
	N	Percent	N	Percent
Ideology				
Social Work is in agency only	9	5.3%	0	0.0%
Psychotherapy is not Social Work	11	6.5%	4	2.6%
Risk Assessment				
Risk is too great	68	40.2%	22	13.9%
Opportunities/Skills				
Lack skills for running private practice	58	34.3%	40	25.4%
Lack physical facility	46	27.2%	3	1.9%
Lack the time	72	42.6%	34	21.5%
Support				
Lack peer support	29	17.2%	5	3.1%
Lack spousal support	8	17.2%	1	0.1%
Other				
	58	34.3%	50	31.5%
Totals	169	225%*	159	100%

*This is a multi-response question

(never to surety), the probability of their engaging in a private practice within five years. As Table 3 reveals, almost two-fifths (39.2 percent) gave low estimates (3 or less), while nearly one quarter (23.1 percent) indicated a high probability (6 and 7). It appears that a substantial proportion will continue to decline a private practice into the foreseeable future.

Reasons for Declining Full-Time Private Practice

Part-time private practitioners, when asked their reasons for not engaging in a full-time private practice, generally gave more than one reason. As Table 4 reveals, their reasons are fairly evenly distributed across the cited dimensions.

A more discerning pattern, however, emerges when respondents were asked for their most important reason for not having a full-time private practice. One-fourth (25.2 percent) wanted to keep a balance between the demands of family and the demands of work. Slightly more than one-fifth (22.5 percent) wanted the financial stability that comes with a regular paycheck. These respondents evidently under-

TABLE 3. Self-Reported Likelihood to Engage in a Private Practice

	(Lo)			(50/50)			(Hi)
	1	2	3	4	5	6	7
	15.4%	12.1%	11.7%	28.3%	9.4%	11.7%	11.4%
N298	46	36	35	84	28	35	34

TABLE 4. Reasons for Choosing Part-Time over Full-Time Practice

	All Reasons *		Most Important Reason	
	N	Percent	N	Percent
Values				
Agency Practice is First Preference	24	16.0%	10	6.6%
Balance Agency w/ Private Practice	49	32.0%	19	12.6%
Balance Work and Family	65	43.0%	38	25.2%
Risk Factors				
Financially Risky	62	41.0%	15	9.9%
Finances				
Keep Employee Benefits	63	42.0%	9	6.0%
Only Want to Supplement Income	53	35.0%	12	7.9%
Want Regular Paycheck	64	42.0%	34	22.5%
Other				
	23	15.0%	14	9.3%
Totals	151	266%*	151	100%

*This is a multi-response question

stand that full-time private practice demands a tremendous investment of time and energy, and are unwilling to sacrifice precious time away from their families and/or to abandon the security of a regular paycheck or the benefit packages that come with agency employment.

Part-time private practitioners were asked to provide an estimate of the probabilities of their engaging in full-time private practice within five years. As Table 5 reveals, about one-third (31 percent) indicated strong probabilities (6 and 7) and about one-third (31.5 percent) indicated weak probabilities (1 and 2). It appears that a sizeable proportion of part-time private practitioners have no intention of entering full-time private practice, and a sizeable proportion harbor dreams of having a full-time private practice. The strength of these intentions and what factors, if any, will influence them in the future are un-

TABLE 5. Self-Reported Likelihood to Engage in a Full-Time Private Practice

	(Lo)			(50/50)			(Hi)
	1	2	3	4	5	6	7
	22.8%	8.7%	9.3%	13.4%	14.8%	16.1%	14.9%
N149	34	13	14	20	22	24	22

known. However, if the proportions hold, agencies can expect to continue to lose more, but certainly not most, of their experienced clinical workers to full-time private practice.

DISCUSSION

The debate over the role and place of private practice in social work will not abate. Arguments against private practice made mostly by social work educators who espouse a restrictive tradition for social work have received wide attention in the literature. In arguing for its containment or elimination, opponents of private practice believe there is an absolute social work historical truth and dismiss private practice as being motivated by crass monetary impulses.

The data, however, suggest that the attempts to convince experienced clinical social workers that private practice is an unholy sapping of the profession's humanitarian spirit may meet with only limited success. An overwhelming proportion of respondents apparently believe that decisions about private practice are more matters of individual choice and governing circumstances, and not necessarily a practice alternative that can be neatly or clearly characterized as ideologically corrupting and mercenary.

Broadly interpreted, the data demonstrate that private practice is not for everyone: a finding that mirrors other studies that suggest that agency-based practice is not for everyone. Clearly, the overwhelming majority of the clinical respondents in this study do not decline a private practice for ideological reasons. Only a very small minority report even including ideological concerns into their deliberations.

Studies that focused on the reasons and motivations of social workers for engaging in private practice have uniformly urged the reform and improvement of agency practice as a way of keeping experienced workers from leaving agencies for private practice. The present data, in uncovering the reasons for declining a private practice, provide another perspective which suggests that many experienced workers will not leave agencies for private practice, despite the persistent problems associated with agency practice, because private practice for them has aspects to it that are even less appealing.

Just as many decline any private practice because it demands time they either don't have or are unwilling to devote, many part-time private practitioners decline a full-time practice because of a desire to strike a balance between the demands of work and the demands of family life. In addition, a sizeable proportion of part-time private practitioners see a value in agency-based practice, preferring it to private practice and/or wishing to strike a personal balance between their agency practice and their private practice. Private practice for them serves supplemental needs and is not viewed as a central focus in their professional and personal lives.

The assessment of risk and one's tolerance for risk figure prominently in decisions about both full-time and part-time private practice. When Freud began his part-time private practice in 1886 he agonized over the economic risks involved in it (Feltham, 1995). In today's managed care environment the level of agonizing has markedly risen. The expense of establishing and maintaining a private practice can be substantial; but the return in income is becoming more and more unpredictable because of the impact of managed care's strong strategies at cost containment and the shifting of financial risk from payers to service providers.

Beyond dealing with the mundane economics, legalities, marketing, and changing structures of private practice (Budman & Steenbarger, 1997; Cummings, Pallak & Cummings, 1996), private practitioners must also deal with the additive stresses typically accompanying the practice of clinical mental health services. Seven "broad overlapping burdens" have been identified as common to all mental health professionals, according to a large literature review by Brady, Healy, Norcross and Guy (1995). These burdens include: (1) distressing client presentations, such as suicidal statements, severe depression, aggression and hostility toward the therapist, and personality patterns; (2) working conditions dominated by a sense of damage, despair, and disease; (3) emotional depletion stemming from the lack of perceived therapeutic success; (4) physical isolation inherent in the privacy of the work; (5) psychic isolation associated with the nature of the therapeutic relationship where the focus is exclusively on the client's needs and concerns; (6) therapeutic relationships that oftentimes result in constant emotional arousal for the therapist in the form of real, painful psychic discomfort from struggles with distortions, unconscious reactions, unresolved conflicts, misinterpretations and antagonisms in relation to particular clients; and, (7) personal disruptions, such as marriage difficulties, serious illnesses, financial concerns, and the stresses of parenting.

It is not surprising that many clinicians will seek to limit the enormous burdens they already shoulder by declining the added risks and loads of a private practice, no matter the power of its allure. As the data suggest, it is precisely because of the risks, the uncertainties, the burdens, and the demands of private practice that many experienced clinical social workers decline a private practice. According to the data, it is not because of any compelling ideological concerns.

On the contrary, the data of this study suggest that the growth trend in the private practice of social work will be affected less by the internal controversies over social work's mission and visions of practice and more by the profound changes in the nature and content of the ever-evolving health care industry.

REFERENCES

Abramovitz, M. (1998). Social work and social reform: An arena of struggle. *Social Work*, 43, 512-526.

Abramovitz, M. (1986). The privatization of the welfare state: A review. *Social Work*, 31, 257-264.

Alexander, M. (1987). Why social workers engage in private practice: A study of motivations and attitudes. *Journal of Independent Social Work*, 1, 7-18.

Austin, D. (1997). The institutional development of social work education: The first 100 years–and beyond. *Journal of Social Work Education*, 33, 599-612.

Barker, R. (1991). Should training for private practice be a central component of social work education? Yes! *Journal of Social Work Education*, 27, 108-111.

Barker, R. (1992). *Social work in private practice: Principles, issues and dilemmas* (2E). Silver Spring, MD: National Association of Social Workers.

Biggerstaff, M. (1995). Licensing, regulation, and certification. In *Encyclopedia of social work*. 19th Edition. (pp. 1616-1624). Washington, DC: NASW Press.

Borenzweig, H. (1981). Agency vs. private practice: Similarities and differences. *Social Work*, 26, 239-244.

Brady, J., Healy, F., Norcross, J., & Guy, J. (1995). Stress in counsellors: An integrative research review. In W. Dryden, (Ed.). *The stresses of counseling in action*. (pp. 1-27) Thousand Oaks, CA: Sage.

Brown, P. (1991). Social workers in private practice: What are they really doing? *Clinical Social Work Journal*, 18, 407-421.

Brown, P. & Barker, R. (1995). Confronting the threat of private practice challenges for social work educators. *Journal of Social Work Education*, 31, 106-115.

Budman, S. & Steenbarger, B., (1997). *The essential guide to group practice in mental health: Clinical, Legal, and Financial Fundamentals*. NY: Guilford Press.

Butler, A. (1992). The attractions of private practice. *Journal of Social Work Education*. 28, 47-60.

Cohen, M. (1966a). The emergence of private practice in social work. *Social Problems*, 14, 84-93

Cohen, M. (1966b). Some characteristics of social workers in private practice. *Social Work*, 11, 69-77.

Cummings, N., Pallak, M., & Cummings, J. (Eds.) (1996). *Surviving the demise of solo practice: Mental health practitioners prospering in the era of managed care*. Madison, CT: Psychosocial Press.

Ehrenreich, J. (1985). *The altruistic imagination: A history of social work and social policy in the United States*. NY: Cornell University Press.

Feltham, C. (1995). The stresses of counselling in private practice. In W. Dryden (Ed.). *The stresses of counselling in action*. (pp. 108-122). Thousand Oaks, CA: Sage Publications.

FitzPatrick, S. & Pardeck, J. (1995). An exploratory study of social workers and psychologists in private practice: Is there a difference? *Family Therapy*, 22, 73-79.

Franklin, D. L. (1990). The cycles of social work practice: Social action vs. individual interest. *Journal of Progressive Human Services*, 1, 58-80.

Gibelman, M. & Schervish, P. (1993). *Who we are: The social work labor force as reflected in the NASW membership*. Washington, DC: NASW Press.

Gibelman, M. & Schervish, P. (1996). The private practice of social work: Current trends and projected scenarios in a managed care environment. *Clinical Social Work Journal*, 24, 323-338.

Goldstein, E. (1996). What is clinical social work? Looking back to move ahead. *Clinical Social Work Journal*, 24, 89-104.

Haynes, K. (1998). The one hundred-year debate: Social reform versus individual treatment. *Social Work*, 43, 501-509.

Jayaratne, S., Siefert, K., & Chess, W. (1988). Private and agency practitioners: Some data and observations. *Social Service Review*, 62, 324-336.

Jayaratne, S., Davis-Sacks, M. & Chess, W. (1991). Private practice may be good for your health and well-being. *Social Work*, 36, 224-229.

Karger, H. & Stoesz, D. (1994). *American social welfare policy: A pluralistic approach*. NY: Longman.

Levenstein, S. (1964). *Private practice in social casework*. NY: Columbia University Press.

McNeece, C. A. (1995). Family social work practice: From therapy to policy. *Journal of Family Social Work*, 1, 3-17.

Perlman, F. T. (1994). The professional identity of the social work psychoanalyst: Professional activities. *Journal of Analytic Social Work*, 2, 25-55.

Richey, C., & Stevens, G. (1992). Is private practice a proper form of social work? No. In E. Gambrill & R. Pruger (Eds.). *Controversial issues in social work.* (pp. 231-238). MA: Allyn and Bacon.

Rubin, A. & Babbie, E. (1993). *Research methods for social work.* Belmont, CA: Wadsworth.

Saxton, P. (1988). Vendorship for social work: Observations on the maturation of the profession. *Social Work, 33,* 197-201.

Seiz, R. & Schwab, A. (1992a). Entrepreneurial personality traits of clinical social work practitioners. *Families in Society: The Journal of Contemporary Human Services, 73,* 495-502.

Seiz, R. & Schwab, A. (1992b). Value orientations of clinical social work practitioners. *Clinical Social Work Journal, 20,* 323-326.

Sheafor, B., Shank, B. & Teare, R. (1998). Unpublished paper delivered at BPD Conference, October 10, 1998: Albuquerque, New Mexico.

Smaller, M. (1987). Attitudes toward private practice in social work: Examining professional commitment. *Journal of Independent Social Work, 1,* 7-18.

Specht, H. (1991). Should training for private practice be a central component of social work education? No! *Journal of Social Work Education, 27,* 102-107.

Specht, H. & Courtney, M. E. (1994). *Unfaithful angels: How social work has abandoned its mission.* NY: Free Press.

Strom, K. (1994a). Social workers in private practice: An update. *Clinical Social Work Journal, 22,* 73-89.

Strom, K. (1994b). Clinicians' reasons for rejecting private practice. *Families in Society: The Journal of Contemporary Human Services, 75,* 499-508.

Strom, K. (1996). The future of private practice. In P. Raffoul & C. McNeece (Eds.). *Future issues for social work practice.* (pp. 97-106). MA: Allyn and Bacon.

Swenson, C. R. (1995). Clinical social work. In *Encyclopedia of Social Work.* (19E). 1, (pp. 502-512). Washington, DC: National Association of Social Workers Press.

Timberlake, E., Sabatino, C. & Martin, J. (1997). Advanced practitioners in clinical social work: A profile. *Social Work, 42,* 374-385.

Trattner, W. (1994). *From poor law to welfare state: A history of social welfare in America.* (5E) NY: Free Press.

Wagner, D. (1989). Radical movements in the social services: A theoretical framework. *Social Service Review, 63,* 264-284.

Wakefield, J. (1992). Is private practice a proper form of social work? Yes. In E. Gambrill & R. Pruger (Eds.). *Controversial issues in social work.* (pp. 222-231). MA: Allyn and Bacon.

Waltz, T., & Groze, V. (1991). The mission of social work revisited: An agenda for the 1990s. *Social Work, 36,* 500-504.

Effects of Managed Mental Health Care on Attitudes of Psychotherapists About Their Work, Their Clients, and the Future of Psychotherapy

Joan Lovell, PhD
Annette Ehrlich, PhD

SUMMARY. Responses by 82 licensed clinical psychologists in California to a 39-item survey (sent to a random sample of 429) showed that fees per hour, number of sessions, and self-rated quality of care all were lower under managed care. Participants reported pressure to terminate quickly and premature termination of treatment by a third party payer. In spite of low morale, most did not intend to leave the field. They had not needed to be retrained for brief psychotherapy, had not altered theoretical orientation and treatment mode from when they first began practice, had not altered diagnoses to fit the requirements of a managed care company, and had not experienced difficulty in becoming providers for managed care companies or in hospitalizing acutely ill patients. *[Article copies available for a fee from The Haworth Document Delivery Service: 1-800-342-9678. E-mail address: getinfo@haworthpressinc.com <Website: http://www.haworthpressinc.com>]*

KEYWORDS. Managed mental health, managed care, psychotherapist, attitudes

Joan Lovell is affiliated with the Department of Psychology, California Graduate Institute (now Newport Beach, California).

Annette Ehrlich is Emeritus Professor, Department of Psychology, California State University, Los Angeles.

Address correspondence to: Annette Ehrlich, 6226 Hollymont Drive, Los Angeles, CA 90068 (E-mail: aehrlich@sprintmail.com).

This article is based on a doctoral dissertation in psychology completed at California Graduate Institute, Los Angeles, CA in 1996 by Joan Lovell.

[Haworth co-indexing entry note]: "Effects of Managed Mental Health Care on Attitudes of Psychotherapists About Their Work, Their Clients, and the Future of Psychotherapy." Lovell, Joan, and Annette Ehrlich. Co-published simultaneously in *Critical Strategies: Psychotherapy in Managed Care* (The Haworth Press, Inc.) Vol. 1, No. 1, 2000, pp. 135-157; and: *Psycho-Economics: Managed Care in Mental Health in the New Millennium* (ed: Robert D. Weitz) The Haworth Press, Inc., 2000, pp. 135-157. Single or multiple copies of this article are available for a fee from The Haworth Document Delivery Service [1-800-342-9678, 9:00 a.m. - 5:00 p.m. (EST). E-mail address: getinfo@haworthpressinc.com].

That managed mental health care is here to stay and is having a profound effect on all individuals who call themselves psychotherapists seems clear (Richardson & Austad, 1991; Sabin, 1992; Schinnar, Rothbard, & Hadley, 1992; Zimet, 1994). What is less clear, however, is the nature of that effect.

Concern has been expressed about the possibility that the emphasis on controlling costs leads to reduced fees for providers and, for patients, a rationing of services (Borenstein, 1991; Schreter, 1993), a decline in the quality of care offered (Karon, 1992; Schreter, 1993; Stern, 1993; Wooley, 1993), and an overemphasis on the use of brief psychotherapy regardless of the needs of the individual patient (Karon, 1992; Wooley, 1993). Experts have suggested that psychotherapists, increasingly, are being forced to stay with previously-approved treatment plans (Stern, 1993) and are having difficulty hospitalizing patients who are in crisis situations (Sederer & St. Clair, 1989; Sharfstein, 1989). Because their options for treatment are being narrowed and they are coming under increasing supervision by third party payers, psychotherapists are said to be suffering from loss of autonomy and a decline in morale (Gabbard, 1992; Hartmann, 1992; Kisch, 1992; Newman & Bricklin, 1991; Sederer & St. Clair, 1989), which may cause many of the best people to leave the field (Wooley, 1993). Further, providers are facing ethical problems not encountered previously, such as, what to do when a case manager or utilization reviewer cuts off benefits at a time when the psychotherapist feels that the patient still requires care (Haas & Cummings, 1991; Stern, 1993).

On the other side, some experts have cited the benefits that accrue, both for psychotherapists and their patients, from managed mental health care. Providers are assured a large volume of referrals and so their incomes go up (Newman & Bricklin, 1991). More patients obtain access to mental health care (Baker & Giese, 1992; Bennett, 1993; Bistline, Sheridan, & Winegar, 1991; Budman & Armstrong, 1992; Giles, 1991; Haas & Cummings, 1991; Hoyt, 1992a; Richardson & Austad, 1991). Quality of care is not decreased if people have short bouts of psychotherapy throughout their lives rather than one long course of treatment (Budman & Armstrong, 1992; Giles, 1991; Haas & Cummings, 1991; Hoyt, 1992a; Richardson & Austad, 1991). As for the need for treatment plans and utilization reviews, it has been argued that psychotherapists need to reeducate themselves so that their treatment plans are realistic and they are able to communicate effectively with people outside the field (Friedman & Westermeyer, 1992; Richardson & Austad, 1991; Zimet, 1994). Finally, ethical problems can be resolved (Haas & Cummings, 1991; Richardson & Austad, 1991; Zimet, 1989); and those people who leave the field are the ones whose personality characteristics make them unable to function under a managed care system (Bistline et al., 1991; Haas & Cummings, 1991; Wellner, 1990) or who persist mistakenly in trying to "change character rather than behavior" (Bennett, 1993, p. 66).

Although much has been written about the supposed effects of managed mental health care on psychotherapists and their patients, there is little empirical data on the subject. An exhaustive search of the literature revealed only four surveys of mental health practitioners. One of these was an informal survey of their readers carried out by the weekly newsletter *Behavior Today* (Martinsons, 1988). Although few details were provided, it appears that respondents thought that the quality of mental health care they were able to provide to patients had suffered under managed care. However, they also reported that they personally had benefited economically due to the increased number of referrals.

A survey of New Jersey psychologists (Moldowsky, 1990) was essentially uninformative since most of the respondents had little contact with the managed mental health care system. A survey of Pennsylvania psychologists (Bowers & Knapp, 1993), carried out only a few years later, revealed a much higher degree of involvement. The two top problems reported were increased paperwork and decreased fees.

Greenwald's (1990/1991) survey was sent to all mental health professionals in California who were under contract to provide services for a particular mental health organization. Overall, respondents seemed to be satisfied with managed mental health care. However, because Greenwald's participants were asked about the agency that employed them, his data need to be interpreted with caution. Respondents may have been reluctant to offer criticism, even on an anonymous questionnaire. There may also have been a self-selection factor with respect to who returned the questionnaires.

It is plain that what is needed at present is more research to determine whether the dire predictions made by some authors have come true. The present study was designed to yield such information. In 1996, a detailed survey was sent to a random sample of clinical psychologists in private practice in California. The intent was to find out: (1) the degree of their involvement with the managed mental health care system; (2) their views about the changes in the profession that have occurred since the introduction of managed mental health care; and (3) how well they are coping with those changes.

METHOD

Pilot Study

A pilot study was carried out in which 10 licensed clinical psychologists who had the PhD degree and were in private practice in California were asked to read and evaluate the items on the questionnaire. Respondents were asked: (1) whether the questions were clear and unbiased; (2) whether the questions appeared to have content validity; (3) whether the entire survey seemed to accomplish the objectives; and (4) whether any questions should be changed, added, or deleted to accomplish the stated objectives of the study.

Nine of the 10 participants indicated that they thought the questions were clear and unbiased. The single participant who responded "no" objected to the response possibilities on a single question. All 10 of the participants indicated that they thought the questions appeared to have content validity and that the entire survey seemed to accomplish the stated objectives. Seven of the 10 participants indicated that they thought no changes were needed. The few changes requested by the other 3 participants were made.

Main Study

Participants and procedure. The survey was carried out during 1996. A letter soliciting cooperation and the survey itself were sent to 429 randomly selected names drawn from a list of the 857 licensed clinical psychologists in both Northern and Southern California who are members of the Division of Clinical Practice of the California Psychological Association. Subsequently, 18 were returned by the post office as *not deliverable*. Another 3 individuals returned blank questionnaires. Seven individuals were not in private practice and could not participate (5 were in forensics, 1 worked for an HMO, and 1 was a college counselor). Another 4 potential participants could not participate because they were retired. The final sample consisted of 82 (53 males and 32 females) licensed clinical psychologists in private practice. The return rate (excluding ineligibles) was approximately 20%.

Survey instrument. The survey,[1] which contained 39 items, consisted primarily of closed-ended questions, the content of which was based on an extensive review of the current literature on the effects of managed mental health care on patients, psychotherapists, and educators.

Information was obtained about the following topics: (1) demographics; (2) the individual's practice, including degree of involvement with the managed mental health care system, fees, and sessions; (3) theoretical orientation and treatment mode, both when the individual left graduate school and at present, and reasons for any changes; (4) quality of care that the respondent was able to offer under managed mental health care and to private patients; (5) specific experiences with managed mental health care; and views about the following: (6) their own futures in psychotherapy; (7) training of psychotherapists; and (8) predicted future trends in the field of psychotherapy.

RESULTS

Demographic Findings

The mean age of participants was 53.8 years (SD = 9.68). The great majority were Caucasian (93.8%). The rest were Hispanic (4.9%) or Asian/Pacific Islanders (1.2%). There were somewhat more respondents from Southern California (60%) than from Northern California. In all cases, the highest professional degree was the PhD. Eleven percent of the sample noted that they also had an MFCC license.

Information About the Participant's Practice

Given the age of the participants, it is not surprising that the typical participant had been in full-time practice for many years (M = 17.2, SD = 8.69). The range was very large, from 3 to 40 years.

The number of patients typically seen per week encompassed a very wide range, from 4 to 55 (M = 25.5, SD = 11.20). Of these, private, self-paying patients were in the minority. They constituted only 26.7% of the workload (SD = 24.8). Patients for whom the provider received reimbursement by a third party payer constituted 71.7% (SD = 25.85) of the total workload. However, there was wide variability. The range for private patients was from 0 to 95%; similarly, the range for patients for whom the provider received reimbursement from a third party was from 5% to 100%.

As Table 1[2] shows, patients were obtained from a variety of sources, the most common of which were *a managed care company, a physician,* and *former patients.*

Table 2 shows the sources that respondents identified as being the ones that provided the greatest and the smallest number of referrals. Although it was assumed that respondents would choose only one source for the greatest and smallest number of referrals, they chose multiple sources, as in the question above. What is noteworthy is that respondents were a diverse lot. There was no single source from which the majority of participants received either the greatest or fewest number of referrals. The three largest sources of referrals were *other* (public and private agencies, attorneys, and advertising), *referral from a managed care company,* and *referral from a physician.* The fewest referrals were received from *other psychologists.*

Rates per hour varied considerably. The range for private, self-pay patients was from $50 to $160, and the range for patients for whom the

TABLE 1. All Possible Sources from Which Patients Were Acquired

Source	Percent
I am a member of a PPO	62.1
Referral from an HMO	54.8
Referral from a Managed Care Company	85.3
Referral from a Physician	85.3
Referral from Other Psychologists	79.2
Referral from Former Patients	86.5
Referral from Schools	30.4
Other (Attorney, Court)	41.4

TABLE 2. Sources from Which the Greatest and Smallest Number of Patients Were Obtained

Source	Percent	
	Greatest Number	Smallest Number
I am a member of a PPO	8.5	8.6
Referral from an HMO	4.9	8.6
Referral from a Managed Care Company	22.0	16.0
Referral from a Physician	19.5	14.8
Referral from Other Psychologists	3.7	23.5
Referral from Former Patients	17.1	12.3
Referral from Schools	1.2	12.3
Other (Public and Private Agencies, Attorney, and Advertising)	23.2	3.7

provider was reimbursed by a third party payer was quite similar; it was $30 to $150. However, the mean rate for private patients was $105.64 ($SD$ = 22.10), whereas the mean rate with a third party payer was only $83.02 ($SD$ = 22.58). The difference between the two means was significant (t [78] = 9.17, p = .000).[3] Respondents earned substantially less per hour when a third party payer was involved.

Respondents indicated the degree to which their rates had changed from 3 years earlier. Table 3 shows the percentage for whom those rates had *increased, decreased,* or remained *unchanged.* Note that the rate had *decreased* for 49.5% of the sample when a third party payer was involved, but it had *decreased* for only 18.1% of the sample when a patient paid privately.

The number of sessions for which a patient typically was seen varied enormously. For private patients, the range was 2 to 300; for patients for whom reimbursement was obtained from a third party payer, the range was 1 to 150. The mean number of sessions was 27.6

TABLE 3. Rate Change from Three Years Ago with Third Party Paying versus Patient Paying

Direction of Change	Percent	
	Third Party Paying	Patient Paying
Increase	5.7	22.9
Decrease	49.5	18.1
No Change	21.0	35.2
Missing Data	1.9	1.0

($SD = 40.88$) with the patient paying and 15.6 ($SD = 23.73$) with third party reimbursement. The difference between the two means was significant ($t[80] = 3.25$, $p = .002$). There were substantially fewer sessions when reimbursement was obtained from a third party payer.

By comparison with the respondent's practice 3 years earlier, the figures for number of sessions represented *no change* for the majority of respondents (55.2%) in the case of the patient paying. However, for the majority of respondents (51.4%), the figures represented a *decrease* in the number of sessions when payment came from a third party payer (see Table 4).

Theoretical Orientation and Treatment Mode[4]

In response to a question about what their theoretical orientation had been when they left school, half of the respondents identified themselves as cognitive/behavioral, and a substantial minority (34.1%) identified themselves as psychoanalytic/psychodynamic (see Table 5).

For the majority of respondents (70.7%), the theoretical orientation had not changed within the last 3 years. For the minority of respondents ($N = 24$) whose theoretical orientation *had* changed, the new theoretical orientation is shown in Table 6. As the table makes plain, the shifts in theoretical orientation have been towards cognitive/behavioral and a theoretical view that supported brief, solution-focused psychotherapy.

Table 7 shows, for the 24 participants whose theoretical orientation

TABLE 4. Change in Number of Sessions from Three Years Ago with Third Party Paying versus Patient Paying

	Percent	
Direction of Change	Third Party Paying	Patient Paying
Increase	1.0	2.9
Decrease	51.4	20.0
No Change	24.8	55.2
Missing Data	1.0	0.0

TABLE 5. Theoretical Orientation When the Respondent Left School

Theoretical Orientation	Percent
Psychoanalytic/Psychodynamic	34.1
Cognitive/Behavioral	50.0
Client-Centered	10.9
Family Systems	7.3
Humanistic/Existential	18.2
Other (Eclectic N = 5, Gestalt N = 3, Feminist N = 1, Erikson N = 1)	12.1

had changed, the reasons for the change. What is noteworthy is that the *need to conform to the policies of a third party payer* was *not* a major reason for a theoretical change. Rather, respondents stated that they had changed theoretical orientation primarily in response to what they perceived as the *patient's needs.*

For 50% of the sample, cognitive/behavioral treatment was either the only treatment mode or one of several primary treatment modes when respondents began to practice (see Table 8).

TABLE 6. Present Theoretical Orientation (Only if Changed)

Theoretical Orientation	Percent
Psychoanalytic/Psychodynamic	12.5
Cognitive/Behavioral	58.3
Client-Centered	4.1
Family Systems	12.5
Humanistic/Existential	8.3
Other (Eclectic N = 5, Brief Solution-Focused N = 5, Transpersonal N = 2)	50.0

TABLE 7. Reasons for Change in Theoretical Orientation

Reason	Percent
Need to Conform to the Policies of a Third Party Payer	20.8
Education	33.3
Patient's Needs	54.1
Other (Integration N = 1, My Interest N = 3, My Dissatisfaction N = 2).	33.3

For the majority of respondents (65.9%), the treatment mode had not changed within the last 3 years. For the minority of respondents (N = 28) whose treatment mode *had* changed, the new treatment mode is shown in Table 9. As the table makes plain, the shifts in treatment mode are in accord with the shifts in theoretical orientation. In both cases, the shifts have been in the direction favored by managed mental health care companies, that is, towards cognitive/behavioral and brief, solution-focused psychotherapy.

TABLE 8. Primary Treatment Mode When Respondent Began Practice

Treatment Mode	Percent
Psychoanalytic/Psychodynamic	29.2
Cognitive/Behavioral	50.0
Client-Centered	9.7
Family Systems	8.5
Humanistic/Existential	18.2
Other (Gestalt *N* = 3, Eclectic *N* = 3, Behavioral/Case Management *N* = 1)	8.5

Table 10 shows, for the 28 participants whose treatment mode had changed, the reasons for the change. The major reason for change was *need to conform to the policies of a third party payer,* but that reason was followed closely by *patient's needs* and other factors. Thus, if the treatment mode had changed it was not entirely due to difficulties with a third party payer.

Quality of Patient Care

Table 11 shows how respondents rated the quality of care they were able to offer their patients under two different conditions–with the patient paying and with a third party payer involved. The overwhelming majority of participants (85.4%) rated the quality of their care as *excellent* when the patient paid, and no one rated the quality as below *good.* With a third party payer, on the other hand, only a minority of participants (23.2%) rated the quality of their care as *excellent.* The majority rated the quality of care as *good* or *fair,* and a small percentage rated their care as *poor.*

Experiences with Managed Care

Respondents were asked to rate how often they had experienced various difficulties with third party payers during the past year. All of the difficulties listed are those that critics have argued would have a

TABLE 9. Present Treatment Mode (Only if Changed)

Treatment Mode	Percent
Psychoanalytic/Psychodynamic	10.7
Cognitive/Behavioral	50.0
Client-Centered	0.0
Family Systems	21.4
Humanistic/Existential	21.4
Other (Eclectic N = 5, Short-Term, Solution-Focused N = 5, Transpersonal N = 1)	39.2

TABLE 10. Reasons for Change in Treatment Mode

Reason	Percent
Need to Conform to the Policies of a Third Party Payer	39.2
Education	25.0
Patient's Needs	32.1
Change in Theoretical Orientation	28.5
Other (Integration N = 1, My Interest N = 1)	10.7

negative effect on care of the mentally ill. Table 12 shows the percentage of respondents who fell into each response category. The two difficulties that a majority of the respondents had experienced *often* were difficulty in obtaining authorization for longer treatment (53.7%) and experiencing pressure to terminate quickly (56.1%). Two other difficulties that a substantial proportion of the respondents had experienced *often* were pressure for a quick diagnosis (40.2%) and the need to be a patient advocate (40.2%). On the other hand,

TABLE 11. Quality of Patient Care with Patient Paying and with Third Party Payer

	Percent	
Rating	With Patient Paying	With Third Party Payer
Excellent	85.4	23.2
Good	14.6	41.5
Fair	0.0	30.5
Poor	0.0	4.9

some situations that critics have said would constitute major difficulties under managed mental health care were only experienced *occasionally* or *never* by respondents. They were: obtaining authorization to hospitalize, consult with other professionals, or obtain psychological testing; pressure to stay with a treatment plan even if conditions changed; and the need to fit the diagnosis to what a third party would allow.

Respondents were questioned about the frequency with which they experienced two other possible problems with managed mental health care. These are problems that have been mentioned in the literature but that are not expected to have a direct effect on patient care. Table 13 shows the frequency with which respondents experienced each problem. Excessive paperwork was reported as occurring *very often* by the great majority (78.0%) of participants, but difficulty becoming a provider was not.

Respondents were asked how often in the last year a third party payer had cut off benefits for patients before the provider felt that those patients should have been terminated. Next, they were asked how they had handled the situation. Specifically, had they reduced their fees or referred the person to a low-cost clinic? Table 14 shows the frequency with which these situations occurred during the last year and how participants responded.

It is plain that the situation in which benefits were cut off prematurely was one with which participants were familiar. Nearly half the sample (48.8%) said that it had occurred *occasionally* and another

TABLE 12. Difficulties with Third Party Payers During the Past Year

	Percent			
Difficulty	Often	Occasionally	Never	Not Applicable
Authorization to Hospitalize	12.2	36.6	18.3	32.9
Authorization for Longer Treatment	53.7	35.4	6.1	4.9
Pressure for Quick Diagnosis	40.2	31.7	25.6	2.4
Pressure to Stay with Treatment Plan Even if Conditions Change	22.0	28.0	46.3	3.7
Pressure to Terminate Quickly	56.1	29.3	9.8	4.9
Need to Fit Diagnosis to What Third Party Will Allow	24.0	54.9	13.4	7.3
Need to Be Patient Advocate	40.2	48.8	6.1	4.9
Authorization to Consult With Other Professionals	9.8	24.4	52.4	13.4
Authorization for Psychological Testing	28.0	28.0	20.7	23.2

TABLE 13. Frequency with Which Respondents Had Difficulty with Paperwork and Becoming a Provider for a Managed Care Company

	Percent			
Problem	Very Often	Occasionally	Never	Not Applicable
Excessive Paperwork	78.0	17.1	4.9	0.0
Difficulty Becoming a Provider for a Managed Care Company	36.6	47.6	12.2	3.7

43.9% said that it had occurred *often.* Slightly more than half of the sample (51.2%) reported that they *often* reduced their fees for such patients. The other options, continuing such patients privately or referring them to low-cost clinics, were resorted to only *occasionally* by the majority of participants.

TABLE 14. Response to Situations in Which Third Party Payer Cut Off Benefits Prematurely

	Percent			
Question	Often	Occasionally	Never	Not Applicable
Frequency of Third Party Payer				
Cutting Off Benefits Before				
Respondent Thought Appropriate	43.9	48.8	7.3	0.0
Frequency with Which Such Patients				
Have Continued Privately	12.2	68.3	17.1	2.4
Frequency with Which Participant				
Reduced Fees for Such Patients	51.2	35.4	4.9	8.5
Frequency with Which Participant				
Referred Such Patients to Low				
Cost Clinics	14.6	52.4	25.6	7.3

Morale and Participant's Perception of Her or His Future in Psychology

When they were asked about the degree to which the advent of managed care had affected their sense of autonomy and morale, the overwhelming majority (84.1%) reported that managed care had had a negative effect on both autonomy and morale.

In response to a question about how optimistic the respondent was about his or her future as a psychotherapist, only 13.4% indicated that they were *very optimistic,* and another 29.3% indicated that they were *somewhat optimistic.* Only a small percentage (4.9%) were *neutral.* The rest were *somewhat pessimistic* (30.5%) or *very pessimistic* (22.0%).

When asked where they saw themselves in 5 years, two-thirds of the sample (65.9%) indicated that they expected to be practicing psychotherapists; the rest (32.9%) indicated that they expected to leave the field or were unsure (1.2%). Of the 27 respondents who definitely expected to leave the field, the largest percentage expected to retire (40.7%), a finding that is understandable in view of the age of many of the respondents, or teach (25.9%).

The data were examined to determine what role age and morale played in the decision to leave the field. The group that planned to stay was compared with the group that planned to leave in 5 years. Morale did not distinguish significantly between those who planned to stay in the field and those who planned to leave in 5 years ($\chi2$ [1, N = 79] = 0.60, p >.05). However, age was a factor. The group that planned to leave in 5 years (M = 59.2, SD = 11.14) was significantly older (t [78] = 3.79, p = .000) than the group that planned to stay (M = 51.2, SD = 7.59).

The Training of Psychotherapists

Because managed care companies limit the number of treatment sessions, there is increasing emphasis on the use of brief psychotherapy. Accordingly, participants were asked whether they had received training in brief psychotherapy and whether, if they could conveniently do so, they would be willing to obtain additional training in brief psychotherapy. The majority (86.6%) indicated that they had received such training. Seventy-two percent indicated that they would be willing to obtain additional training. Given these figures, it would seem that the low morale reported by participants was not the result of inability to use a treatment technique that is favored by managed mental health care companies.

An additional question that was asked with respect to brief psychotherapy was whether participants would be less willing, in the future, to accept patients who, in their view, would not benefit from brief psychotherapy. Only a minority (32.5%) responded affirmatively; the rest answered negatively, which means that they would be willing, in future, to accept patients who, in their view, would not benefit from brief psychotherapy.

A series of questions were asked about the adequacy of training in graduate school to handle various aspects of managed mental health care. Table 15 shows how respondents rated their training. It is plain that respondents thought that they had not been adequately trained in a number of areas. Given their age and years of experience, that lack of training is not surprising. More than half the sample rated their training as *very poor* or *none* in the following areas: obtaining reimbursement, obtaining authorization to hospitalize a patient, obtaining permission for additional treatment, and dealing with the ethical problems involved when the patient's needs conflict with the policy of the managed mental health care company. Only in the case of setting behavioral goals for treatment did a majority of respondents rate their graduate training as *very good* or *good*. This highly negative assessment of

TABLE 15. Ratings of the Adequacy of Graduate School Training to Deal with Various Aspects of Managed Mental Health Care

	Percent			
Aspect	Very Good	Good	Poor	Very Poor or None
Writing Treatment Plans	9.8	14.6	35.4	40.2
Obtaining Additional Treatment	2.5	2.5	33.3	61.7
Obtaining Reimbursement	1.2	0.0	26.8	72.0
Obtaining Authorization to Hospitalize	1.2	8.5	25.6	64.6
Use of Brief Psychotherapy	14.6	22.0	32.9	30.5
Ethical Problems	6.2	17.3	22.2	54.3
Setting Behavioral Goals for Treatment	25.6	41.5	13.4	19.5

TABLE 16. Suggested Changes in the Present Educational System

Suggested Change	Percentage
No Change	8.5
More Emphasis on Brief Psychotherapy	70.7
Training in How to Write Treatment Plans	79.2
Training in How to Be a Patient Advocate	78.0
Training in How to Work with Case Managers	73.1
Training in Technical Details Involved in Obtaining Reimbursement	75.6
Training in How to Deal with Ethical Problems	70.7
Other (Business Practices and Marketing $N = 8$, Legal Issues $N = 4$)	24.3

the adequacy of graduate training may have to do with the fact that the average participant's age was 53.8 years, which means that many had gone to graduate school before the advent of managed mental health care. This fact was duly noted by a number of respondents on their questionnaires.

Participants were asked what changes in the present educational system they would suggest. They were instructed to check all of the ones that they deemed appropriate. Very few participants favored the *no change* option. An overwhelming majority (70% or more in all cases) endorsed *all* of the possible changes listed–more emphasis on brief psychotherapy, training in how to write treatment plans, training in how to be a patient advocate, training in how to work with case managers, training in the technical details involved in obtaining reimbursement, and training in how to deal with ethical problems. Of the participants who chose *other,* the largest number ($N = 8$) saw a need for training in business practices and marketing skills. Other possibilities suggested were legal training ($N = 3$), a cessation on training psychologists, training in "creative prevarication," training in a brief form of psychodynamic therapy, redefining psychology away from mental health, and training in computer-assisted therapy ($N = 1$ in each case).

Future Trends in the Field of Psychotherapy

Respondents were asked about their degree of agreement with two ideas that have appeared in the literature on managed mental health care: (1) that psychotherapists need to give up their emphases on "cures," and (2) that patients should be seen for short periods at crisis points rather than for a single, extended period. Seventy-one percent favored the idea of giving up on cures but only for some, not all, patients; another 19.8% thought that the idea should not be applied to any patients. Ninety-two percent favored the idea of seeing patients for short periods at crisis points rather than for a single extended period, but again with the reservation that the idea applied to some but not all patients.

Participants were asked their degree of agreement with two statements that often are made about the future benefits of the present trend toward managed mental health care. The first statement was: "In future, more people will benefit from mental health care." The majority (64.6%) disagreed strongly and another 17.1% mildly disagreed. The second statement was: "In future, more attention will be paid to the prevention of mental illness." A smaller majority (53.7%) disagreed strongly, and another 15.9% disagreed mildly, but there was a substantial minority (19.5%) that expressed mild agreement.

DISCUSSION

The results showed that a number of negative predictions that have been made by critics of managed mental health care have indeed been realized for psychologists in California. Fees per hour and number of sessions allowed are lower, and clinical psychologists feel that the quality of care they can offer under managed care is not as good as what they offer to private patients. A number of specific problems were reported: excessive paperwork, difficulty in obtaining authorization for longer treatment, pressure to make a quick diagnosis and to terminate quickly, and premature termination of treatment because benefits were curtailed by the third party payer. Not surprisingly, morale is low, feelings of autonomy have decreased, and there is considerable pessimism about the future.

The results also showed that not all of the negative predictions made by critics of managed mental health care have been realized. In spite of low morale, the majority of participants did not intend to leave the field; those who did intend to leave within the next 5 years planned to retire. The extensive retraining of clinical psychologists so that they can do brief, cognitively-oriented therapy that had been predicted by some experts (Giles, 1991; Richardson & Austad, 1991) does not seem to have occurred. Most participants had not changed their theoretical orientation and treatment modes from those they had favored when they first began practice. Although they were willing to receive additional training, they reportedly had used cognitive techniques since they left graduate school. They had not experienced difficulty in any of the following: becoming providers for managed care companies, obtaining authorization to consult with professionals, hospitalizing acutely ill patients, or obtaining approval for psychological testing. The majority had not altered diagnoses to fit the requirements of a managed care company, and they had not experienced pressure to stay with a treatment plan if conditions changed.

Some issues could not be adequately resolved. The plan was to carry out comparisons between groups of psychotherapists with different theoretical orientations and treatment modes in order to determine whether their opinions and experiences differed, but it was not possible to do this because, even though respondents were asked to choose the *primary* theoretical orientation and the *primary* mode of treatment, many respondents chose more than one. Consequently, it was not possible to establish clearly-defined categories of psychotherapists. It would be of interest to determine, in a follow-up study, whether the practitioners with the lowest morale and the greatest number of reported problems with managed mental health care are the ones whose primary theoretical orientation and primary treatment mode is psychoanalytic. The reason for suggesting that such may be the case is that, of all the treatment modes, it is psychoanalytic treatment that seems to lend itself least readily to brief, crisis-oriented psychotherapy (Budman & Armstrong, 1992; Hoyt, 1992a).

Because participants made more than one response, a similar problem arose in analyzing the data on the sources from which respondents obtained the greatest and smallest number of referrals. This is an issue that could be clarified in a follow-up study. Finally, more research would be needed to investigate the adequacy of graduate training to deal with the problems that arise in conjunction with managed mental health care. In this study, the typical participant was middle-aged and had received her or his graduate training before the advent of managed mental health care. If a follow-up study were conducted, it would be useful to obtain a sample that was composed only of recent graduates.

One conclusion to be drawn from the data is that changes need to be made in the education of clinical psychologists. Graduate students should be taught the specific skills necessary to work within a managed mental health care system: obtaining reimbursement, functioning as a patient advocate, writing treatment plans, and using brief methods of psychotherapy. It may be that, as some experts have argued (Hoyt, 1992b), less emphasis should be placed on training graduate students to use treatment techniques that focus on insight and analysis.

Another conclusion to be drawn from the data is that clinical psychologists need to take some action on their own behalf. Through their state and national organizations, they need to lobby for whatever changes in the managed mental health care system are necessary to ensure that patients continue to receive quality care and that access to such care is not severely limited (Sederer & St. Clair, 1989). They need to find a way, as suggested by Zimet (1994), to become active in managed mental health care decision-making groups. By doing so, they will work from within the system and not from outside. The goal should be to ensure that it is psychologists, and not business persons, who make the decisions about who is covered, for how long, and for what kind of treatment (Hoyt, 1992b). Finally, as suggested by Gabbard (1992), clinical psychologists need to learn more about how the decisions of managed mental health care companies can be appealed and also the appropriate agencies to which abuses can be reported.

Taking such action will be therapeutic. It should help clinical psychologists to regain some of their lost feelings of autonomy. If they feel more autonomous, morale should improve, and perhaps clinical psychologists will feel less pessimistic about the future.

NOTES

1. A copy of the survey is available upon request.

2. Because each participant listed multiple sources, the percentages shown total to more than 100%.

3. An alpha level of .05 was used for all statistical tests.

4. For all of the questions in this section, it was assumed that respondents would make one choice. However, they often made more than one. Consequently, the percentages shown in Tables 5 through 10 add up to more than 100%.

REFERENCES

Baker, N. J., & Giese, A. A. (1992). Reorganization of a private psychiatric unit to promote collaboration with managed care. *Hospital and Community Psychiatry*, *43*, 1126-1129.

Bennett, M. J. (1993). View from the bridge: Reflections of a recovering staff model HMO psychiatrist. *Psychiatric Quarterly*, *64*, 45-75.

Bistline, J. L., Sheridan, S. M., & Winegar, N. (1991). Five critical skills for mental health counselors in managed health care. *Journal of Mental Health Counseling*, *13*, 147-152.

Borenstein, P. (1991). Managed care: A reply. *Hospital and Community Psychiatry*, *42*, 320.

Bowers, T. G., & Knapp, S. (1993). Reimbursement issues for psychologists in independent practice. *Psychotherapy in Private Practice*, *12*, 73-87.

Budman, S. H., & Armstrong, E. (1992). Training for managed care settings: How to make it happen. *Psychotherapy*, *29*, 416-421.

Friedman, S., & Westermeyer, J. (1992). Psychiatrist case managers. *Hospital and Community Psychiatry*, *43*, 648-649.

Gabbard, G. O. (1992). The big chill: The transition from residency to managed care nightmare. *Academic Psychiatry*, *16*, 119-126.

Giles, T. R. (1991). Managed mental health care and effective psychotherapy: A step in the right direction? *Journal of Behavior Therapy and Experimental Psychiatry, 22*, 83-86.

Greenwald, M. D. (1990/1991). *Attitudes and patterns of practice of mental health professionals working under a managed care system.* Unpublished doctoral dissertation, California School of Professional Psychology, San Francisco, CA.

Haas, L. J., & Cummings, N. A. (1991). Managed outpatient mental health plans: Clinical, ethical, and practical guidelines for participation. *Professional Psychology: Research and Practice, 22*, 45-51.

Hartmann, L. (1992). Presidential Address: Reflections on humane values and biopsychosocial integration. *American Journal of Psychiatry, 149*, 1135-1141.

Hoyt, M. F. (1992a). In a health-maintenance organization: Some information for private practitioners. *Psychotherapy in Private Practice, 11*, 47-53.

Hoyt, M. F. (1992b). Discussion of the effects of managed care on mental health practice. *Psychotherapy in Private Practice, 11*, 79-83.

Karon, B. P. (1992). Problems of psychotherapy under managed health care. *Psychotherapy in Private Practice, 11*, 55-63.

Kisch, J. (1992). Psychotherapy: Dilemmas of practice in managed care. *Psychotherapy in Private Practice, 11*, 33-37.

Martinsons, J. M. (1988). Are HMOs slamming the door on psychiatric patients? *Hospitals, 62*, 50-56.

Moldowsky, S. (1990). Is solo practice really dead? *American Psychologist, 45*, 544-546.

Newman, R., & Bricklin, P. M. (1991). Parameters of managed mental health care: Legal, ethical, and professional guidelines. *Professional Psychology: Research and Practice, 22*, 26-35.

Richardson, L. M., & Austad, C. S. (1991). Realities of mental health practice in managed care settings. *Professional Psychology: Research and Practice, 22*, 52-59.

Sabin, J. E. (1992). The therapeutic alliance in managed care mental health practice. *The Journal of Psychotherapy Practice and Research, 1*, 29-36.

Schinnar, A. P., Rothbard, A. B., & Hadley, T. R. (1992). A prospective management approach to the delivery of public mental health services. *Administration and Policy in Mental Health, 19*, 291-308.

Schreter, R. K. (1993). Ten trends in managed care and their impact on the biopsychosocial model. *Hospital and Community Psychiatry, 44*, 325-327.

Sederer, L. I., & St. Clair, R. L. (1989). Managed health care and the Massachusetts experience. *American Journal of Psychiatry, 146*, 1142-1148.

Sharfstein, S. S. (1989). The catastrophic case: A special problem for general hospital psychiatry in the era of managed care. *General Hospital Psychiatry, 11*, 268-270.

Stern, S. (1993). Managed care, brief therapy, and therapeutic integrity. *Psychotherapy, 30*, 162-175.

Wellner, A. M. (1990). Some thoughts on the future of the professional practice of psychology. *Professional Psychology: Research and Practice, 21*, 141-143.

Wooley, S. C. (1993). Managed care and mental health: The silencing of a profession. *International Journal of Eating Disorders, 14*, 387-401.

Zimet, C. N. (1989). The mental health care revolution: Will psychology survive? *American Psychologist, 44*, 703-708.

Zimet, C. N. (1994). Psychology's role in a national health program. *Journal of Clinical Psychology, 50*, 122-124.

Index

Action, as stage of change, 65-66
Adolescent(s), mental health services for, 74
Agency for Health Care Policy and Research, 65
Alcoholism, managed care and, 82
Allen, J., 82
American Managed Behavioral Healthcare Association (AMBHA), 27
American Psychiatric Association (APA), views on managed care, 75
American Psychological Association (APA), resistance to defining differences in psychologists' functioning in managed care by, 15-16
American Psychological Association's (APA) Code of Ethics, in provider's responsibility, 7
American Psychologist, 44,45
American taxpayers, managed care effects on, 20-21
Apgar, D.H., 87

Behavior Today, 137
Behavioral managed care organizations (MBCOs), 21-37
Benedict, J.G., 72
Berman, W.H., 65
Blau, B., 110
Brady, J., 131
Brickman, P.M., 95
Buyers Health Care Action Group, 33

Children, mental health services for, 74

Clark, W., 107-108
Code of ethics, described, 88-89
Code of Ethics of the National Association of Social Workers, 88-89
competence in, 92-95
confidentiality in, 97-99
conflicts of interest in, 95-97
developing written practice guidelines for managed care in, 102-103
establishing peer ethics committees in, 102
informed consent in, 90-92
interruption of services in, 99-103
privacy in, 97-99
self-determination in, 90
social workers' ethical responsibilities to their clients, 90-193
termination of services in, 99-103
Cohen, B., 1
Competence, in Code of Ethics of the National Association of Social Workers, 92-95
Confidentiality
in Code of Ethics of the National Association of Social Workers, 97-99
described, 106
effects on patient self-disclosure, 105-120
history of, 107-108
impact of managed care on delivery of psychological services in, 12-13
Confidentiality law